5 . 2006

'The Bull' is originally published in *Cages and Other Stories* (Lime Tree Press, 2006).

'Raw' is the winner of the Yorkshire Arts Circus Short Story Competition 2006.

Published by The Writing School, Department of English
Manchester Metropolitan University.

September 2006

Copyright ©

Printed and bound in England by MMU Media Services

ISBN (1-905476-10-8)
       (978-1-905476-10-7)

Manchester
Metropolitan
University

CONTENTS

SKY

Nicola Scargill

"Tell me about the sky," she said, and her eyes were round and sweet, home to two million stars; and her lips dripped honey diamonds onto a sparkle of ash and narcotics. There was no sky that day, just a plaster maze of nicotine and flies, listening to her corn syrup voice whisper its lullabies to a deaf city. Her walls were close, inches off her starved angel's face; martyr's face; an offering to the god of all the little things no one else would ever notice, too jaded to bother; and 'tell me about the sky.'

My sky floated, wrapped around me; security; a mist of everything I'd loved and lost, bought, sold or remembered, everything I'd learned, earned or hurt for since the bottom fell out of the sour world. I bit my lip, caught it carefully and held; gently coaxed a single drop of red copper and oxygen from its pink velvet taste, old wound remembered by the warps in oily red lipstick and happy to bleed for a minute, to breathe again.

"What if the sky should fall?" And my own voice soaked the air up, fine and creamy notes strung between us like a blood tie; and she frowned, her soft brows dipping over violent eyes, little mirrors with humanity seeping into the cracks, grime set in deep and dirty layers, cloudy and distorting. I had a picture of a sky like patchwork with a big ragged hole in the middle, loose threads and the tattered patch clinging to the whole, one seam caught in the tangled spread of colours and cotton, and I sat back and stared up into the cracks and chips stretched out over my head.

What would fall out of the hole?

A Sea View

I choose the rocky ground,
whilst she plays in the shallows.
She likes the waves, 'So blue,'
but never stays until the sun goes down,
when it purples the view like bruising,
bringing tears to the eye of the evening.

She swims in the ponds,
protected from the stormy tides.
My pond was full of tiddlers
swallowing stones and
crashing into the sides,
getting tangled in the weeds.
They flounder without feet to stand
and float lifeless to the surface.

The sound of snapping jaws
trembled through the still.
I prayed for a net to catch me.
Drowning in the murky dark,
I dripped with silt and sorrow
that stagnated my fishy heart.

But this fish will not be free
in those see-through waters.
I'd prefer to taste the gritty salt
than live in that sugary sea
where only the honoured cod can breathe,
whilst entire shoals lie gasping on the shore,
all dried up and unable to speak.

Alison Jeapes

THE WOMAN IN THE STREET

Glenis Stott

I saw a woman in the street and feel compelled to tell her story. It isn't the story I would choose to tell. That story would be as lazy as a lullaby, sliding from my fingers to the keyboard in a restful rhythm. But the choice is not mine and I'm forced to write using pen and paper, the words rushing from my mind to be scratched out onto the page.

I don't know where the story will take me. I only know the woman's story in the way that we all know others' stories, the details varying but the basic facts remaining the same. I have a beginning; a woman, younger than me, shopping alone in the street, her face creased with anxiety, her knuckles white from the heavy bags she carries, but it's not really the beginning, for I neither know nor understand how that woman came to be there, on that day and at that place.

I tried to follow her, on that hot summer's day, threading my way through other shoppers, but she was soon lost to my sight. She stayed in my mind though and now, late that same night, I've taken up my pen to make words from the images that sprang to mind as soon as I closed my eyes and tried to sleep.

Her early childhood, I think, was in a world much kinder to her than this one. There was sunshine warm on her face. I don't know the name of the place but it was somewhere the girl (I think I'll call her Susie) could run free, chasing orange butterflies and singing nursery rhymes. Perhaps it was a farm, or a whitewashed cottage. Or even a caravan where money was short but life was happy. The idea makes me smile and I put down my pen to think what memories she must have of that time.

But then, pfff, the bubble bursts and my pen is in my hand again. There was unhappiness. Suddenly. A death. The father? No, the mother. The woman who made the home a happy place, gone. Disappeared from this child's life. No time to prepare. A heart attack, late at night. Or an undiagnosed tumour, eating away at her inside until there was nothing left. Next morning there was no one there to make breakfast. Susie doesn't know what it was; all she knows is that she is alone. Or almost alone. There is the father, formerly a smiling, outgoing man, now cold and distant, who can't look at his child without seeing the newly-deceased mother. Maybe she would be better without this man, packed off to stay with a white-haired grandmother who smells of lavender and bakes bread. The girl could recover with the grandmother, could learn to sing again. But there is no grandmother, only an icy father freezing everything he touches. Especially Susie.

This is not the way I want the story to go. How can I leave Susie alone in that caravan (it was a caravan) with this man? I've never met him and yet his presence is here in the room with me, making me reach for a wrap to put around my shoulders. If I could get her out I would, but there's nowhere else for her to go.

I don't want to do this. I won't do this. I rip the page from the notepad, crumple it in my hand and toss it, like a snowball, into the corner of the room.

I return to bed but sleep is slow to join me. My body is as cold as stone and, behind my eyelids, solitary figures curl up like question marks. When I finally sleep my dreams are frigid and barren.

Next morning I'm angry with the woman in the street for her interference in my life. I vow to leave her to her fate. I sit at the computer where I earn my living tapping out stories for others to read. Out of the corner of my eye I can see the paper snowball that holds Susie at its centre. Once or twice I go to pick it up and throw it away but I don't touch it because I don't want to play any further part in Susie's sad life.

The words won't come. The place in my head where I find my stories is like a snow covered landscape, everything white and frozen. I have to deal with Susie so I can get on with my own life. I pick up the paper and lay it on my desk, smoothing it as best I can. My pen hovers over the page as I build up the strength to go on. As the nib touches the paper, it begins to race across the crumpled surface.

Susie's now called Sue. Her life seems better. She's in her teenage years. Still in the caravan but the father has thawed a little. Sometimes he even smiles. She's doing well in school and there's an English teacher who's taking an interest in her, helping her with her work. She's started writing. She enjoys writing stories, controlling her characters, making them do what she wants. I remember that feeling. Now my character is controlling me. It's not a good way to write.

But wait. The teacher, a man, has an ulterior motive. It's not her writing that he's interested in. And I can't stop it, however hard I try. The snowball rolls down the hill, growing bigger until it happens. He makes his move and then moves on.

Back in the caravan Sue is silent and downcast. The father is confused. "What have I done?" he asks. Sue shakes her head and draws the thin curtain around her bed. The father blames himself. He hasn't been a good father. He slides back into his ice shell, never to emerge again.

Sue lies on her bed staring up at the ceiling, trying to explain what happened. Maybe she looked at the teacher in the wrong way. Or said something provocative. Or perhaps it was in her writing, something that said she needed to be loved. She knows it has to be her own fault.

How did I get involved in this mess? My writing meant everything to me and now it's tainted, made dark and dirty by my entanglement with some stranger in the street. I have to pull back, get away before I'm dragged further down into someone else's problems. I leave the room and try to get on with my life. Go out. See friends. Like I did before. Except, of course, it isn't the same because I no longer have my writing.

Time passes. The limited income I used to receive from my stories has gone. I find another job, selling tickets in the local cinema. At the end of my shift I slide into the soft darkness and watch other writers' stories play across the screen. Sometimes there are happy endings, sometimes not. Still, however hard I try, I can't forget Sue. She's with me when I sit in my little booth handing out tickets. I wake in the night gasping for breath from dreams of her in that claustrophobic caravan.

My health suffers. I develop asthma and my skin breaks out into strange rashes. The doctor becomes concerned. He prescribes me inhalers and lotions and refers me to Dr Galbraith.

Dr Galbraith makes a tower of his fingers and rests his chin on the top. He says, "There are many parallels between your life and Sue's. You're drawing them out in your story and that's why it's so painful." He's wrong. I'm very different from Sue. My mother is alive and well. Living in Scotland, I think. My English teacher was a woman and I can't remember chasing orange butterflies as a child.

He goes on. "You control the pen – you can control the story and what happens to Sue. If you don't take control, then you will degenerate even further."

The man is a fool and I tell him so. He's never held a pen and scrawled out a story in this way. He doesn't understand me. I leave his office and don't return.

Back home I go to my study and carry on with Sue's story. I have no choice.

Sue meets a man. A man who brings her single red roses and takes her for walks down by the river. They set up home together in a dark house which she brightens by painting the walls in vibrant colours. Lilac for the lounge. Scarlet for the bedroom. They share cosy meals in the cramped kitchen and talk late into the night. She's happy for the first time in a long time.

I'm happy too. I can leave Sue and focus on my own life. I also find a man. He brings me bright bunches of flowers and takes me to restaurants where the air is heavy with garlic. We share private jokes and try to spend all our time together.

One afternoon when he's working and I'm at home alone, I venture into the study. Sue's story lies on the desk in a patch of sunlight. I pick it up and read it. I wonder what happens next. I take up my pen and begin to write.

It's not good news. Her man no longer gives her roses; he only gives her babies. One, two, three babies. She loves them but life is hard, there's little money and every day is a struggle. The walls that she painted with bright colours are now faded and stained; sometimes they close around her like a straitjacket.

He comes home one evening. "I've found someone else," he says. "She laughs with me. She listens to what I say and makes me feel good." He packs a bag and leaves. Sue isn't surprised. What else could she expect?

The next day, out shopping in town, she feels as though someone is watching her. It's not a new feeling, it's been with her on and off throughout her life. But this day it's really strong. She hides around a corner and her fears are confirmed. She sees a strange woman pushing her way through the crowd, eyes darting from side to side. Then the stranger stands, shading her eyes with her hand and gazing around her in bewilderment.

This is all the confirmation Sue needs. She dashes home. After collecting the children from the neighbour's, she closes the front door firmly and barricades herself in her bedroom. The children cry and knock on her door; they are tired and hungry and they want their mother. Their voices intrude on her thoughts; she wishes they'd be quiet. She puts her hands over her ears and begins to scream.

This is too much. Why is this woman such a victim? She has her children, why isn't she standing on her feet fighting for them, instead of huddling in the corner of a locked bedroom? I have no patience with Sue or her story. Pushing the pages into a drawer, I lock the study door and go out for a walk. It's late and the streets are deserted. I walk quickly through pools of yellow light cast by street lamps. I find myself down by the river.

I sit on a cold wooden bench and watch the moving distortions of the moon on the water's surface. An image flashes into my mind. An image of that dank water closing over my head, silver bubbles escaping to the surface. It's more than an image. I can feel my hair wafting in the water like seaweed. I can feel the cold probing deep into my heart.

I have to get back to Sue. I can't leave her alone. I hurry back through the deserted streets. My chest becomes tight and several times I have to stop to catch my breath. When I arrive at the house my skin is damp and my hair clings to my forehead. I drop my coat on the floor and return to Sue.

She's in a place where the lights are too bright. She doesn't know where she is nor how she got there. Someone tells her the children are being looked after. I wonder what happened? Maybe the neighbours called Social Services about the noise. Or maybe their father came home to collect some things to find his children distressed and alone. Whichever it is, we're glad her babies are safe.

Strangers in white talk to her incessantly. They tell her when to eat and when to sleep. They ask her questions she can't answer. One day someone hands her a pen and some paper. The pen is cool in her fingers. The paper is smooth under her hand. She fills the pages with stories. A white-haired grandmother bakes bread in a farmhouse kitchen. A young girl chases orange butterflies through long grass. When she's finished each story, she pats the pages with satisfaction.

After time it's decided that she is fit to leave and they find her a small flat. Contact is arranged with her children. The children are taller and thinner and smell of someone else. Her daughter sits in the corner and sucks her thumb, refusing to speak. The older son climbs on her lap and hides his face in her neck. The younger talks about his other mummy and tells stories of treats and trips to the park. When the time comes for parting, both she and the children find it so painful that she says she doesn't want to see them any more.

She paints the walls of her flat in lemon and puts plants on the windowsills. She writes in the mornings and searches for bargains in the market in the afternoon. The nights are almost painless and life is almost satisfactory.

And then, one day, she sees a woman in the street.

THE VOICE

Mike Dugdale

John closed his eyes and took a deep breath. The sweat on his forehead mixed with the layers of foundation on his face and produced a smell like sweaty almonds. The lights above were hot and he felt thirsty. The name was Sissay. He opened his eyes and stared into the crowd.

"I'm getting a name," he said. "A foreign name." He pulled the most sincere frown he could muster. "Sissay. Does the name Sissay mean anything?"

There was an audible gasp from his left. He turned to face it.

"*Benjamina Sissay.*" Caroline's voice crackled through the receiver in his ear. It was small and concealed just inside the ear canal. "*To your far left. A black woman, come with her three daughters. She's wearing a red blouse.*"

John located the family straight away. They were the only black faces in the crowd.

"I'm getting the name Benjamina." He looked straight at her. "That's you, isn't it?" He pointed and she nodded. The spotlight focused on her. People never questioned that. It somehow never occurred to them that the man who operated the spotlight found his targets so quickly. It was all down to planning and organization. Caroline was good at that. His career had taken off since he married her.

"Please Benjamina, stand up."

The woman gripped the arm of her chair and rose to her feet. She towered over the rest of the aisle. She was overweight and her hand continued to hold onto the arm of the chair. That meant she was unsteady on her feet. She must have problems with her health. He guessed she was in her forties. Her hair was short and frizzy and her skin was beginning to show deep wrinkles. The blouse and skirt were cheap, possibly from Primark, probably even more downmarket. Perhaps she had money problems as well.

"Don't be shy," he told her. "The spirits are with us every day. There is nothing they don't already know about us."

He tried to remember what Caroline had shown him about the woman. The audience had been full of rich pickings that night and he'd had a lot of profiles to read through. The night had been a huge success so far. The Sissays were to provide a bang towards the end of the show.

"*Her son, Nwankwo, died in a traffic accident two years ago,*" Caroline told him. "*He was 19 at the time.*"

John remembered the newspaper cutting he'd read before the show. Benjamina's son had died at an accident black spot not far from his home. The newspaper had been campaigning for the introduction of speed bumps. There had been a picture of Nwankwo next to the article. He was wearing a blue T-shirt and blue and orange baseball cap. He'd been wearing them on the night of the accident.

"I'm getting a young, male voice and a name. Please forgive me if I pronounce this wrongly. Nwankwo? Does that mean anything to you?"

The woman's face fell into her hands. One of her daughters stepped up to the spotlight and embraced her mother. She rubbed her eyes with the palms of her hands.

"He was your son, wasn't he?"

"Yes," the woman said.

"He's telling me about a car. He says he didn't see it coming. He was run over, wasn't he? He says he wishes there had been speed bumps on the road."

The woman let out a low moan. She shook her head.

John smiled. "He's told me to tell you not to cry. He's happy now. He says he's still got the hat. He's saying something about a blue and orange hat."

"A baseball cap," the woman said. "It was his favourite. He wore it everywhere. He was wearing it when he died."

"*Good, John,*" Caroline told him. "*It's his birthday next week. You're doing well. Now start to wrap it up.*"

"He says he's happy you've come here tonight. He's asking you not to forget his birthday."

"I won't," the woman said. She pulled her hands away and looked at John. Her eyes were swollen and puffy. She sniffed and reached for her daughter's hand.

"He says not to get upset over him. He's happy where he is and he's watching over you. Thank you for coming."

The woman shook her head and started to cry again. The spotlight pulled away from her. She sat down.

John scanned the room. There was one more person he planned to speak to. George Brechin was somewhere in the audience. He was an elderly man with combed over white hair and glasses. John liked him. He regularly attended John's shows and sometimes even paid for private consultations. He always seemed so moved by John's words. His wife's death had left a giant hole in his life. Occasionally, John would try to fill it.

John's gaze skimmed over the crowd. He saw the young, well-dressed woman whose mother had recently died from cancer. She had been his first contact that night. Then he noticed the man in his early fifties. When John first saw him he looked like a pub doorman. He was still crying, even now, convinced he had just spoken to a father who had been uncommunicative in life. John's eyes passed over a woman in the third row.

"*Bitch!*"

John stopped. It was a man's voice.

"*Bitch! Bitch! Bitch!*"

John rubbed the side of his face. The foundation stuck to his fingertips. He pressed them against the receiver in his ear.

"*Go to George Brechin,*" Caroline said. "*He's right in front of you. In the first row.*"

"*Bitch! She's a bitch!*"

The voice was harsh and unfamiliar. It growled at him like a threatening dog. John felt a pain in the middle of his chest. The voice wasn't speaking to him through the receiver.

He looked for George Brechin. He saw the woman staring at him.

"*Pick her.*"

The woman leant forward. She placed her hand against the top of her chest and swallowed.

"*Pick her. Pick Annette.*"

"*John, what's wrong?*" Caroline said.

The pain in his chest increased. He bowed his head and rubbed the bridge of his nose. It was the distress signal. John had left a plant in the audience. If the show was going badly, he would simply rub his nose and the plant would respond to whatever name John uttered next. He had never had to use her since he'd met Caroline.

"I'm … I'm looking for Annette."

The plant raised her arm. The woman on the third row blinked. John lifted his hand and pointed to the plant at the back of the room.

"*No! Pick Annette,*" the voice told him.

John's chest tightened. The pain spread to his arm. He pointed to the woman in the third row.

"You're Annette, aren't you?" he said.

The woman stood up and nodded. The spotlight fumbled around the audience until it fell on her. She seemed frightened by the attention.

"*John, go back to the plant,*" Caroline told him. "*We don't know anything about this woman. She bought her ticket at the door.*"

John relaxed his arm. He pulled on the collar of his shirt and opened the top few buttons. The lights felt hotter than ever.

He stared at the woman. She was small and thin and had short, greying hair. He got the impression she had come on her own. She was wearing an expensive black trouser suit and looked to be in perfect health. He guessed she was in her late fifties. He wondered who she had lost.

"*She's a bitch! Tell her Harry says she's a bitch!*"

"I'm getting the name Harry. Does that mean anything to you?"

The woman gasped. She brought her hand to her mouth. John noticed the wedding ring on her finger.

"Harry's my husband," she said. "He passed away last year."

"*She's a whore. She cheated on me. Tell her I was there when she fucked him.*"

"He says he's watching over you," John said.

"Oh my God!" The woman held her head in her hands. A tear rolled down her left wrist.

"*You're not doing what I tell you!*" said the voice. "*Tell her I laughed when he beat her. Tell her she deserved it – she's a bitch!*"

John's chest tightened. His forehead was hot. His left arm felt light and there were pins and needles in his fingers. He was breathing rapidly now. He wanted to lie down.

"He says that you've been in a troubled relationship recently. He says he doesn't like to see you upset. He still loves you."

The woman moved her hands from her face. She blinked and swallowed hard. Then she smiled.

"*Bastard!*" the voice said. "*Bastard! Bastard!*"

John closed his eyes. He felt close to fainting. He tried to breathe, but his chest seemed to be fighting against him. He bent over. His heart stopped beating. He fell to the floor.

"*John!*" he heard Caroline scream.

He awoke in a hospital bed. The room was dark and he shivered in the cold. He turned on his side and tried to pull the blanket over his shoulder. It didn't move. It was folded, tightly, under the mattress.

John wondered how he had got there. He remembered the young woman who had lost her mother. He remembered the man who looked like a bouncer. He remembered the black woman whose son had died in a car accident. He remembered the voice.

Caroline would be furious with him. He'd deviated from the plan. Cold reading she could permit, but how would he explain the voice? He didn't understand it himself. He guessed he'd had some kind of heart attack. He thought he'd read somewhere that stroke victims often hallucinated when they had their stroke.

"Caroline?" he said.

There was no answer. He tried to sit up, pulling at the blanket where it folded under the mattress. The chair by the side of the bed was empty.

"Caroline?"

He rubbed the tops of his arms. He couldn't seem to get warm. He dangled his feet from the end of the bed and pushed them against the floor. There was a door ahead of him. He walked towards it. He couldn't see much in the darkness, only what the light seeping through the glass allowed. As he got nearer, he was able to see through the window. Caroline was arguing with a doctor. They were walking towards him. He tapped against the glass.

"Caroline!"

"I want to see him," he heard her say.

The doctor pushed open the door. John stepped back. A light flickered on in the room.

"Caroline. I'm here."

They walked past him. John followed them with his eyes. They stopped by the side of the bed. John gasped. He saw his own body lying white and prostrate. He fell to his knees and wept.

"John," Caroline said. Her voice faltered as she spoke. "Please don't leave me."

She turned away from the bed. She swallowed the lump in her throat and cried into the palms of her hands.

The doctor placed his arm around her shoulder and escorted her out of the room. The door closed behind them. The light flickered off.

"*She's a bitch!*"

John looked in the direction of the voice. A man stepped out from the darkness. He was short and bald and as white and lifeless as John had been on the bed.

"*She'll cheat on you,*" the man said. "*They always do. They're all bitches!*"

Early March. An easterly wind scrapes my face. We find a bench, face west.

"What did she say?" you demand.

A cloud of starlings splinters above us. How can I explain that she pulled me down, kissed my mouth like she was eating a soft mango?

I turn the paperweight over in my pocket, inside it, a dead flower. Imagine us smashed into pieces on the ground, petals and leaves everywhere.

"I never said it was forever," I answer, words that snatch you away, clutching your pelt, as they take flight.

A siren in the distance moans, salvage operation.

THE PAPER CRANE MAN: ICHI (ONE)

Katy Harrison

When he was born they thought there was something wrong with him because he was so unnaturally still. The midwives snatched him away and prodded and poked him until eventually he did cry and was handed to his father, a perfect squalling baby. Nothing had been amiss; he just hadn't felt like crying. His parents, though, named him for his first few moments: Kiyoshi, meaning 'quiet.'

    Kiyoshi Arakaki was born on 7th October 1933, in the city of Hiroshima in the Western Honshū region of Japan. His mother was from the same city, but his father was from Okinawa, the principal island in the Ryūkyū Archipelago, which was at that time independent from mainland Japan. Here his father, Hirokazu, had studied *karate*, and was able to do so freely as the ban on the art was lifted just before he was born. Up until that point it had been forbidden for 300 years. Knowledge, secrecy and honour were among the most prized things in his country and accordingly Hirokazu had educated his young son from an early age in *Karate-Dÿ*, the Way of the Empty Hand.

    Hirokazu had left Okinawa to attend university in Hiroshima, where he had met Sonako Yamamoto. She hadn't been a student; she had been helping her grandmother on one of the stalls in the market place and had met Hirokazu when he was shopping for a gift for his then girlfriend. The gift was forgotten; they got engaged a few months after and married when Hirokazu left university. Kiyoshi came along nine months later.

    Sonako practiced *jo-jitsu,* the elegant martial art that employs the use of a short staff, the *jo*, in its moves. Some of Kiyoshi's earliest memories were of his parents training together, silently practising their moves and then breaking into giggles as his father scooped up his mother and spun her around. They had a practically unheard of relaxed relationship behind closed doors, but in public his mother wore formal *kimono* and walked behind her husband in his salaryman suit. It was the way things were expected to be.

'Right, Kiyoshi. That was better, but show it to me again, *desu*?'

    Kiyoshi, dressed in loose fitting clothes like his father, bowed sharply from the waist. He breathed deeply and the heavy smell of cherry blossoms in the garden drifted into his nostrils.

    '*Taikyoku Shodan*.' He announced the name of the *kata*, the pattern, he was about to perform for his father and moved into the *yoi*, ready position. Under the watch of his father he performed the 20 moves, focusing on his technique. When he completed the *kata* he brought his feet together and bowed.

    'That was good. Do you think you know that *kata* then, Kiyoshi?'

    '*Oss.*'

    'Really *really* know it?'

'…*Oss.*'

'Show me it backwards then.'

Kiyoshi's face faltered for a moment. Then he picked up his concentration and performed the *kata* backwards, although slightly slower than before. His father nodded.

'Now two-steps-forward-one-step-back?' he said, meaning that after every two moves the participant performs the last move backwards. It was a common test to see how well a *karate-ka* knew his *kata*. Kiyoshi looked stricken. 'I'll do it with you then.'

Together they performed the *kata*, Kiyoshi twisting his face fiercely so that he wouldn't get tangled up or fall behind his father's pace. Gradually Hirokazu increased the pace and Kiyoshi battled hard to keep up. At the end a flustered Kiyoshi finished a millisecond behind his father. It was then that he realised his father was grinning and he grinned back. Normally karate was not so light-hearted, but when it was just the two of them Hirokazu couldn't bear to be hard on his son.

'You shouldn't smile during *kata*, *Sensei*.'

Sonako's voice teased them. She had been watching them during their training and now approached the pair of them.

Kiyoshi and his father bowed to end the *kata* and to each other.

'True, but an *otou-chan* can.' Hirokazu smiled at his wife, using the word for 'daddy'.

Kiyoshi watched as his father swept his mother off her feet, ignoring her shrieks and carried her into the house. He followed, running. He could smell oysters, the speciality of Hiroshima, and *soba,* thin buckwheat noodles, mixing with the cherry blossoms. Inside the house he could hear his parents laughing.

6th August 1945 07:59:36, Hiroshima, Japan

The sunrise that morning had been so clear that the early morning traders remarked on it in the streets. The sky was free of clouds and the sun reminiscent of the Japanese flag.

Kiyoshi was late rising for school and his mother rushed around trying to cajole him into his uniform. Finally he was in his white shirt, blue jacket, blue shorts and blue cap. His mother packed *onigiri*, a rice sandwich with *nori*, seaweed, on the outside, with pickled plums for a filling, into his bag for a snack at break time and they began the walk to school.

As they walked the *ginkgo* trees shaded them from the heat that was already setting in. A rogue female tree's yellow berries gave off a noxious smell and they hurried past. They followed the path lined with the waxy white flowers of the *senninsoo* plant into the hub of the city which was a mixture of concrete, bicycle bells, paper lanterns, students, soldiers and army vehicles. Living a short way outside of the centre of the city afforded Kiyoshi and his family the benefit of countryside and trees and flowers. Sometimes late at night they could forget the city was there. When they could do that they could sometimes forget about the war as well.

As they entered the main part of the city an air raid siren cut through the air.

Joining the sudden thronging crowds, Kiyoshi and his mother tucked themselves into a shelter to await the all-clear. This was not uncommon when an American B-29, *B-san* they called it, was sighted in the skies so they were not unduly worried.

Minutes later the all-clear was sounded and a man with a megaphone announced that it was safe to come back out. Instantly the city picked up where it had left and people continued their journeys to work and to school.

They arrived at the school building and Kiyoshi and his mother went in. The classroom began to fill up with other students and their anxious parents. Rumours over what the Americans would do next occupied the adults' thoughts and made them uneasy over leaving their children.

Kiyoshi's mother reached out to straighten her son's cap. He grinned at her and then pushed her hand away when he heard other boys giggling. Recognising one of the boys, Kiyoshi went to join a game of tag they were about to start. To decide who would be 'It' they started a round of *Janken*, the Japanese version of Rock, Paper, Scissors. With expressions of little-boy seriousness they chanted as their fists rose and fell.

'*Janken, Janken, Pon!*'

Watching her son, Kiyoshi's mother smiled sadly as she understood that this was the first step toward losing her little boy.

'*Janken, Janken –*

08:15:00

'*– Pon!*'

The next moments in Kiyoshi's life were silent. A magnesium flare, the *pika-don*, and then everything turned white as the sky went out.

A fat coil of smoke rose into the sky.

The cloud began to form over to the west of them and everyone in the building stood still at the windows, hypnotised, trying to work out what it was.

'*Kiyoshi!*' his mother screamed his name, grabbed his hand and pulled him under a table with her.

Then the blast rushed in and blew out the windows over their heads and they knew.

08:17:05

Kiyoshi could hear people screaming. It took him a few moments before he realised that he was one of them.

The skin of most of those around him looked torn and shredded, red and angry. He recognised it as burns, but burns didn't kill people, he reasoned.

The room smelt of grilled dried squid and it made him feel hungry until he matched it up to the sight of the seared flesh of others. He vomited and then looked around.

Everything that hadn't been bolted to the floor was strewn about as though a clumsy child had knocked over a doll's house.

The heat was all around them, inside of them. Kiyoshi's mother pulled her son to his feet.

'Kiyoshi! We have to be quick. Do you understand?'

He had nodded, but he hadn't really. His mother grabbed him again by the hand and they ran with other desperate people, past clusters of groaning bodies. Hands grasped at detached limbs, the dead locked together in positions of protection, their arms covering their faces. Those who hadn't been able to get under cover as the blast hit were burnt raw from head to toe, their skin hanging in tatters. They screamed for water and they screamed for their mothers. They reached out with blistered hands and Kiyoshi yelped when one closed around his ankle. He wrenched his leg free and ran after his mother.

They made it to the street and had barely seconds to catch their breath when someone shouted a warning – *'Abúnai!'* – and the building collapsed behind them as the floors fell in on each other one by one.

What glass was left in the windows now burst out and scattered the people in the street. Kiyoshi reached up to touch his head and his hands came away red. His mother pulled him to her and then her legs went out from beneath her and she was sobbing in the street. Above them the light of the morning was replaced by a depthless black cloud; not even the sun survived what had happened.

Kiyoshi looked at his mother and saw that her arms and hands and one side of her face was burnt. He looked at himself. Apart from the blood from his head he was relatively unscathed. There were patches of sore skin on his arms where his mother's cradling hadn't quite covered, but if that was the extent of his injuries then he considered himself lucky.

08:28:41

As they sat in the street the rain began to fall.

The moisture covered the upturned faces of Kiyoshi, his mother and the other survivors and they opened their mouths to the water. They saw that the droplets were black and big, so big that they hurt when they landed on them. Thick and sticky, the uranium in the atmosphere had turned the rain into a poison and now it was bathing their bodies and soaking into their clothes.

Fires broke out simultaneously in the city. Beneath the roar of flames clamouring for oxygen was the sound of thousands of people crying.

Two girls huddled on the steps of the library that blazed behind them, making no move to run for safety, because there was no such place.

Children without parents sobbed and coughed in the smoke.

Men shouted for help as they tugged survivors from the wreckage of once-proud buildings. Those who could still walk helped the trapped out from underneath sheet metal and heavy crumbled bricks.

The sky was now burnt black and screams filled in the gaps between shouts for help and broken buildings. Kiyoshi and his mother crouched in a doorway and watched as the dead and the dying intermingled, collapsed on one another until they were indistinguishable, interchangeable in his mind. His mother gripping him so tight that he would later find marks, Kiyoshi surveyed the necropolis that was now their city and now their world.

9th August 1945

Kiyoshi's mother died three days later.

She complained of being hot all over and her burns never healed. They festered and began to smell. She was tired all the time, and could barely move to comfort Kiyoshi when his own injuries made him cry out in the night. When she began to vomit blood they knew she had the sickness internally. It was swift, barely letting them puzzle over one symptom before another appeared.

When she died it was only her and Kiyoshi. He curled up next to her and waited. For a long time he just thought she was sleeping since she had been doing a lot of that recently. But when she began to go cold, he knew.

He left his mother's body in the building where they had sheltered and stumbled around the city. He was still dressed in his school uniform which was by now dirty, ragged and bloodied. Exactly whose blood it was was now uncertain, because every person he had come into contact with, every surface he touched was covered in blood and soot.

The fires had begun to abate as the army moved through the city, extinguishing the worst and rescuing the people able to be rescued. As Kiyoshi picked his way through the ruined city he concentrated on the thought of his father. Kiyoshi knew he worked at the Prefectural Industrial Promotion Hall and began to make his way toward it. All around him buildings lay flattened as if they had been nothing more than houses of cards. The smell of death was inescapable as bodies lay in carbonised mounds, their skin stripped from the flesh, unrecognisable as human beings.

Kiyoshi followed the Motoyasu River, which had more bodies in it than water, up to the Promotion Hall. What greeted him was not the ornate structure from three days ago, but a wasted dome with crumbled walls and blown-out windows that resembled a skull, hollow and anonymous.

The sickness felt stronger here and Kiyoshi felt nauseous. His body began to feel hot all over and, as he realised that he should get away, he collapsed.

The narrative goes on to follow Kiyoshi through the years as he is taken in by his aunt and uncle and struggles to come to terms with what has happened. What follows is an extract from later in the story.

6th August 1975, 21:17:57, Kibune, Japan

Kiyoshi's uncle had a stack of paper to one side of him and his hands made quick movements as they manipulated the sheet in his lap. A perfect *origami* crane appeared from the folds of the paper and Kiyoshi's uncle placed it on the floor in front of them.

'Do you know what that is?'

'A *tsuru*.'

'And why do we fold them?'

Kiyoshi began to answer and then closed his mouth and looked away to the west. His uncle tried a different tack. 'Do you know who Sadako Sasaki was?'

Everyone knew who Sadako was. Two years old when the atomic bomb was dropped, she had developed leukaemia nine years later. A friend who visited her in hospital told her of an old Japanese legend about the crane, a bird who lives for a hundred years, and that a person who folded a thousand paper cranes would have a wish fulfilled.

Sadako began folding *origami* cranes in the hope that when she had folded the thousandth she would be cured of her illness. She folded 644. After her death at the age of 12 her friends continued to fold the rest, in the hope that peace would come. Since then every year thousands of brightly-coloured cranes are folded by both children and adults and placed at the foot of the Children's Memorial on the anniversary of the Hiroshima bombing. In Japan cranes are the ultimate symbol of hope, of peace, of longevity. To give or receive a crane is to give or receive the wish that peace can come to us all, that hope can continue to exist, that we should continue to live.

'So, you understand?'

Kiyoshi nodded.

'And you understand that at the age of 12 she never gave up? That she believed that peace and hope would someday come?'

'Sadako died.'

'Yes, she did. Like your mother and father. But you are one of the lucky ones. And even though you shake your head now, you still have life. That is more than most.'

'But what kind of life is this?'

'Every life is precious.'

'Why doesn't it get any easier?'

'You're a grown man now, and a man knows that life is not fair, and he does not argue with it.'

'Cranes won't un-make what happened. They don't change a thing.'

'…They might shape what will happen. It is only in the shadow of death that we find life.'

Kiyoshi didn't reply.

The sun was beginning to set and his uncle stood up, picked up his tea and walked back into the house. Kiyoshi continued to sit with the stacks of paper and the solitary crane, facing west, the direction of Hiroshima.

Extracts from a longer story.

Diving

In the summer, we are starved
achieving sinewy, sweat-born perfection.

Heat holds our tongues,
replacing hunger with lethargy.

We seek solace
in cool, dark lake water.
Breaking the surface,

we emerge streaming and lithe,
float on our backs,
propelled,

Then dive down, finding the middle
watery place between glass top
and silt bottom.

Not knowing up from down,
caught in liquid purgatory,

centre of the earth's womb
we are caught by our ankles,
bound by umbilical vines.

We are born into air,
our heads come up and
suck in the afternoon.

Squinting,
our eyes
against the sun.

Sarah Hardman

Gillian Appleby

'At the moment things are custard and later they will probably turn into christmas pudding but maybe if you're around at 2 we can talk.'

Taking up his metaphor she writes: 'My days are more like liquid.'

She asks if he wants to meet.

'U cld be a physcho,' he messages.

She wonders if he has mistyped or just can't spell.

Dominic, the green-eyed IT man from downstairs, a ring on his left hand twinkling evilly at her, asks if he can show her something on her computer. Something drops inside her stomach. He starts clicking and a screen pops up asking if she'd like to talk to Nirvanarashid. He disregards and continues. She looks at him. There is nothing on his face but concentration. Luckily the new programme he wants to show her isn't working and he goes to another computer on the other side of the room. Quickly, her hands shaking, she tells charlesjudd she has to go and closes all the 'personal' windows.

Later, opening up the chat window again, charlesjudd writes about the woman he wants. 'She's got to be confident and independent – not clingy!'

Then he writes she must like, 'a but of "dinner satisfaction".'

What is he referring to here?

She replies: 'Abitofdinnersatisfactionorabutofdinnersatisfaction?'

Her space bar won't work. He tells her to get a knife and lever it up.

'No need it's working now.'

The space bar keeps going on and off like a dripping tap.

'Do you smoke?' he asks.

To be cool she writes, 'Tobacco – no.'

'So are you a weekend toastie? I'm an evening puffer and a weekend toastie.'

She wonders if he is purposefully trying to confuse her or whether he actually talks like this. She asks what he means but there is no reply.

She logs in every two hours and starts logging in at home, in the evenings. charlesjudd disappears for a few days. She looks for others to chat to at work but no one interesting answers her questions. Faces begin to look the same. She looks through several pages and stops when she is on page 21. She has looked at 210 men.

By the afternoon she feels oppressed. Opening the windows doesn't help nor does the fact that the others feel it too. Some of them have been working there for years. One of the guys is leaving soon – migrating to New Zealand with his Kiwi wife. She feels a peeved jealousy seep into her mind every time she thinks of it.

charlesjudd is back.

He gives her his mobile number and tells her to text him sometime. She doesn't think she will but thinks of things she could say.

'hey charles are u as crazy as I think u r?'

'hey charles what ya doin?'

Of course she has to drop full words. Writing them whole would make her seem serious. Less flippant – like she wants him.

He is just a picture. Even with the e-mails and 'chats' he is not real. She would have to meet him for him to become alive.

The next day charlesjudd isn't there. She sees other guys with nice pictures. Beginning to feel impatient she e-mails five of them. One replies. He thinks he might be too tame and boring for her. He's training to be a barrister. She thinks he might be right.

Someone e-mails her – his name is 'James or Jamie – see how easygoing I am?' The conversation goes something like this:

'what would you wear on a date with me'

'jeans, boots, a vest top'

'what would you wear underneath?'

'underwear'

'r u a thong or knickers girl?'

She doesn't answer.

* * *

Easygoing, down to earth, decent, confident, sexy, good looking, sporty – these are the catchwords of this cyber-dating world. She doesn't want to have to say she is any of these things. At first, she had drawn a blank when trying to come up with a description of herself. But you couldn't be on the site without it so she had said she liked the cinema, cafés, drinking, talking till two am, having a laff. All the things that had been said countless times. She was relying on her photo to do some of the talking for her.

Couples surround her on the tube. One person gets up; two people sit down – inevitably touching each other.

She gives charlesjudd her number halfway through a chat the next day at work. Minutes later her phone rings. It's him. Such a strong accent – he asks her if he can call her when he gets home. She feels the whole room listening. Wonders if they can hear him talking because he is so loud on the other end.

There is a buzzing in her mind when she gets off the phone. She finds it hard to remember what she was doing.

He doesn't call in the evening. She carries her mobile around the house with her. Lays it down, goes into another room, comes back, picks it up. The same screen stares back at her.

He texts her the next day saying he got home late. Replying to her reply he texts, 'Can't help thinking your a "nice" girl who wants 2 reach out and b touched. I think your charming and would love to meet u.'

She texts him back: 'How bout meeting nxt Wednesday?'

There is another guy who starts chatting to her. Calls himself timbucki. His name is Sam he tells her. He wants to meet but his profile is hidden. He wants to keep his details secret. She asks if he has a photo.

The photo is black and white. He's wearing a suit and tie, a wedding picture. Not his – he says 'he he.'

'so when we gonna have our date?'

She is shocked at the pressure he is putting on already. But he doesn't look too bad. She says she is busy this week. They make a day next week. She gives him her number.

Friday evening. Oxford Street. Black streets. Red, yellow, green bleery lights. Her phone vibrates and rings. A private number makes her heart lurch.

'Hello, this is Sam.'

'Oh hi.' She can't believe the cheek, but manages to speak.

'Let me do an intelligence test on you.'

She fears what's coming.

'What colour is snow?'

'Is this a joke or something?'

'No.'

'Okay it's white'

'What colour are the clouds?'

'White.'

'What do cows drink?'

'Milk… No that's not right. We drink their milk but they don't drink milk.'

'That was a bit slow but you got it right.'

Throughout this conversation her battery is beeping at her. Suddenly it gives two beeps and dies. She looks at it and feels a sense of being let off a very large hook. Saturday afternoon. The absence of work calms her. She is watching a late night movie she recorded. The house is empty except for her and the TV.

Her mobile starts to ring. She has saved charlesjudd's number so she knows it's him. She looks at the phone for a few rings, cannot decide whether to pick it up. But it seems stupid not to.

'Hello.'

'Hey this is Charles.'

'Oh hello.' The hello rings out high pitched – her mother's voice.

'What are you doing tonight? Because there's this party in Kensington a whole bunch of people I know are going to. Just wondered if you wanted to come too.'

'Sounds a bit heavy,' she says instantly regretting it.

Her ear hurts he's so loud. Must be in a street somewhere.

'So you're just going to have a quiet evening in?'

'Yeah I think so.'

'Okay then.'

He starts to tell her about how he's in Covent Garden wearing flares and it's just poured it down and water has got trapped in his flares, and now he's going home to dry out.

'You talk very fast.'

'Well I'll make a mental note of that for Thursday.'

'Wednesday,' she corrects him.

She puts the phone down. Feels like a fool. Disastrous conversation.

'You talk very fast.' Why did she say that? Why didn't she ask him more about the party? She should have been upforit. She doesn't go to parties anymore. She feels like an old woman. She has lost out on charlesjudd – she knows it.

***

Monday at work, barrister man has e-mailed asking if she would like to meet him. She says yes.

He is late. She stands with her stomach in her mouth in Angel station searching people's faces. When they look at her she blinks away. Surely he will recognise her.

After half an hour he does. She realises his photos must have been quite old. His receding hairline wasn't part of her imagination. They go to a pub nearby and she can't think of a thing to say. She is starting to have the worst regrets – her panic thoughts taking over, disabling her mouth. He doesn't talk – waits for her to entertain him. She has a glass of red wine to help her out: to loosen her tongue, her brain. Instead it helps to loosen her bowels. She sits on the toilet for at least ten minutes. It is only 8.30.

She goes back to the table and says she feels unwell.

'Unwell? You look fine to me. Have another drink…'

She feels burdened. She says she is sorry, she must go. He walks her to the station. He tells her some people from his work are drinking around the corner. Letting her off or lying, she isn't quite sure.

At work on Tuesday there is an e-mail waiting for her from barrister man. He says he had a good time. Did he think she had? She deletes it.

* * *

She writes to a guy called Roamer who wants to travel the world, Azzran – she queries him over his name, Bretzy – whose picture has a blue sky behind him, Peri who is Australian.

A Turkish guy e-mails her and asks her if she wants a friend in Turkey. A Nigerian guy tells her he would like to 'engage in serious a relationship with her,' if she doesn't mind. A 55-year-old called fitanfun asks if she would like to date someone older.

By the end of the week there is no word from charlesjudd.

She realises none of the guys she has e-mailed are going to reply.

She doesn't renew her subscription.

She consistently searches the internet for entertainment but finds nothing. She logs onto another dating site and finds that although the men are different essentially they are the same. They use their real names but there are just as many fakes.

West of the Lizard

The Lizard is an area of Cornish coastland.

The lizard roared, baring cockled teeth, as the boy scaled its spine,
Waves snashed as they feasted on the land.
Lantern thrust to his front and a mule at his hind,
Half a groat buried deep in his hand.

"Fare thee well my Juliana!
Heave away me jolly boys, we're all bound away,
'Tis black and we hear those gulls a-callin'
From the rocks on the perilous bay."

Perched on the mount, gale-swayed and salt-cracked,
Washed in flame, the boy haunted his post.
Jewelling the mist, an *ignus fatus* in the black,
Tempting bleary eyed jack-tars to the coast.

"These strange waters will surely claim us boys!
Less a watchtower lights our way.
Storm a-long! The horses'll call us down,
And on the bed of the sea we'll stay."

No lighthouse to angel these shore.
Only villagers to creep with bloodied hands,
To plunder the men above whose heads roar,
The waves that sweep their treasures to the sand.

Jessica Greaves

Blackface

The gentlemen seated and ladies folded,
Children clean-faced and suitably scolded,
Under canvas, sun-bleached and coarse.
The air thick with beasts, a soft floor of mire,
Old glory overhead, flagging and tired.
Jim jumps in his crippling fourths,

And saw-dusted feathers, giving their wearers no flight,
Bleed gasps from their watchers at awe-gusted heights,
The painted faces still baying for more.
Roll up Mr Tambo, knuckles cracked from chipping stone,
And another just like him, swapped his hammer for bones.
Wear their faces to a musical score.

Ragged in the ring, plucking strings in quickstep time,
Dancing for corn far from the field, fresh on the dime.
Plantation ghosts stalk in the wings.
The captain reined their fathers, now the trammel's holding strong
Whispers in the ear, the deep down drum of working songs
And Coal Black Rosie sings.

Tucked under the curtain, hushly waiting for his cue,
Creasing by the fire sits this troubadour of hue.
Hears applause from hands that once spurned.
Hears crowing from a crowd so falsely snicker glutted,
They laugh at only ink as the face was born as sooted,
And the cork is slowly burned.

Jessica Greaves

SEVEN CURSES

Helen Brown

I. Old Reilly Stole a Stallion.

Beneath the star-speckled night sky, a troubled man struggled to fall asleep. It wasn't the cool evening air, or the flickering fire beside him, but rather what he had done which disturbed his mind. The whining of the stallion, which was bound to the bough of a tree in front of him, served as a constant reminder. His aged face contorted as he wrestled with his conscience. A moment of madness meant he had now ruined any possibility of freedom and when he was discovered, he would be punished mercilessly, for there was no hope for a black man.

The fugitive's nightmarish thoughts about his impending fate were suddenly dispersed as he felt the cold, metal barrel of a shotgun press against his temple. Opening his eyes he saw the shadowy figures of 20 or more men, each almost as indistinguishable as the trees which surrounded them. A jagged pang of fear pierced his stomach; if he tried to run now, he'd be dead within seconds. As he slowly raised his hands above his head, the figures remained motionless for what seemed like an age, until the silence was shattered abruptly by their crude, sonorous laughter.

With this, one of the figures stepped forward so that the light of the fire illuminated his rough, weather-beaten features which were etched with malevolence.

He paused as though to allow the fugitive to gauge his opponent, before arrogantly continuing his advance until he towered above his captive. He paused a second time, savouring the moment. As the fugitive defiantly met the gaze of his looming captor, it became obvious that the savage laughter had stopped. The atmosphere within the tight circle of men was so intense that the ragged old man's spine seemed to buckle under its weight until he folded forwards, letting his spittle cover the boot of his opponent. In the same moment a blinding pain engulfed his upper body as that same boot connected with his mouth and nose. And then other boots joined in, his body became numb and, finally, darkness overwhelmed him.

II. Old Reilly's Daughter Got a Message.

The hot sun was beating down upon Rosa Reilly's back as she held the parasol over her mistress' head. Her neck was scorched and sweat flowed freely down her face whilst she fought to keep her aching arm outstretched. Still, it was a far more favourable position to be given than those of other girls. Despite the kindness of her employers, she couldn't help longing for more. She had been separated from her father on the Jefferson farm just outside Montgomery, Alabama four years previously so that she could wait on another white family in Selma. Servitude was all she had known, but without her father by her side it was no longer easy; she was miserable now, and no amount of comfort could change that.

Rosa's fond daydreams of being with the only family she had were consistently interrupted by her mistress' commands and enquiries,

"Rosa, have you gone slow? You're getting the sun all on my face again – hold it up girl."

"Sorry ma'am."

"Yes, yes, it's not your fault you're slow, just don't do it again or I'll send you inside." While her mistress, Miss Abernathy whined, Rosa rolled her eyes with impatience. She certainly wasn't slow, but that was the popular consensus held by most white people. Perhaps she had just as much or more sense than Miss Abernathy, who, at 12 years of age, was considerably younger than Rosa. Just as her thoughts had drifted back to life in Montgomery, she was distracted again, but this time it was by her mistress' father who strode towards her with a stern expression upon his face.

"Rosa, I've just received a little news concerning your daddy down at the Jefferson's. Would you like to accomp'ny me to my study?"

"Yessir," stammered Rosa, as she felt a rush of excitement swell in her stomach at the mention of her father. Was he to come to Selma too? As she followed Mr Abernathy into his large colonial house, Rosa heard the angered squeals of his daughter calling after him,

"Daddy, who's gonna hold my parasol now? Give me back my maid! Daddy!"

Once inside the swelteringly hot study, Rosa waited at the door while her employer seated himself behind his desk and then beckoned her forward to the chair in front of him.

"Now Rosa, it is my understanding that your ol' pappy has got himself into a spot of bother with the law down in Montgomery." Mr Abernathy's lazy southern drawl couldn't sooth the anxiety that rapidly replaced her previous excitement. "I've just received word of his arrest following an attempted escape from the Jefferson's and theft of one of George's finest stallions." Rosa's breathing quickened, as she felt her throat begin to tighten. She understood what this meant for her father. "I'm afraid he's going to be hanged in two days. I'm gonna allow you to go to him before his execution; you may use one of our horses." His voice was gentle, yet the tone managed to betray his lack of concern on the subject.

"Th-thank y' kindly sir." Rosa spoke quietly, not quite believing what she had heard. She had dreamt almost every night since their separation that some day she would be allowed to return.

"That's all right Rosa, you can leave later – but for now I believe I can hear my daughter hollering." He gave her a benign smile and then leant over the paperwork upon his desk. Rosa mumbled her thanks again before shuffling out of the room. When she stepped outside, her tears went unnoticed as her mistress demanded that she held up the parasol again.

III. "The Price, My Dear, Is You Instead."

At nine o'clock that night, when the Abernathy family had retired to bed, Rosa Reilly prepared to embark on her 20 mile journey to Montgomery on one of the family's oldest horses. There was little in her satchel except for that which she intended to bargain with: she had stolen one of Mrs Abernathy's pearl necklaces and some of her rings when the rest of the household had been eating their supper. After checking the jewellery was still by her side, and contemplating for just a moment whether theft would be as damning for her as for her father, she dug her heels into the horse's sides and galloped ahead onto the dusty track which would lead her to Montgomery.

It was a cold and damp morning that greeted Rosa as she approached Montgomery. The streets were quiet but she knew her father wouldn't be asleep. However, she hadn't come to say a farewell to her father, but to rescue him, and that meant dealing with the man who put him there. Her first destination was the Courthouse; an intimidating building that struck fear into the hearts of Montgomery's inhabitants. It certainly had that effect upon Rosa as she pushed one of its enormous wooden doors, her hands trembling with the unease that swelled in her stomach. Inside she was told that the man responsible for the handling of her father was a judge named John Mather, but the informant was of no further help other than to warn her that she shouldn't entertain any hope of changing his mind.

Judge Mather's office was not unlike Mr Abernathy's. His desk was of similar proportions: large, and made of a thick, dark wood. The occupant also chose to surround himself with hundreds of books and globes. Rosa guessed that it was most probably to give the impression that he possessed a superior intellect. However, it became immediately clear that Mr Abernathy and Judge Mather were two very different men. As he admitted her into his office he greeted her with a smile which caused her heart to begin pounding within her breast. There was no kindness in his eyes, but rather an imperious stare, which seemed all the more derisive as his lip curled.

"Now what would a pretty young thing, such as yourself, be doing in a place like this, I wonder." The sarcastic, cruel tone in his voice sent a shiver coursing through Rosa's body as he stared at her with his piercing blue eyes.

"M-my name is Rosa Reilly, sir. I was told that you'd … ah … taken care of my father, William Reilly, s-sir." She was mindful that like many of the white men she had met, she would have to show the respect he demanded.

"Ah, you mean Old Reilly. My my, he must be very proud of his daughter. Beautiful. Quite beautiful indeed… He is to be hanged tomorrow, of course."

"That's what I came to speak with you about, sir." Rosa summoned her courage from deep within her heart as she knew this was her only opportunity. "I've come to beg for his life. Here, I've brought gold and silver…" Her voice broke as she looked pleadingly into his face, tears already burning in her eyes.

That lecherous smirk began to spread across his face once more as he took in every curve of her body. "I don't want your money," he laughed. "The price, my dear, is you instead."

IV. In the Night the Price was Paid.

Her father was dismayed as he listened to his daughter's story. She was so hopeful that she might save his life, but he could never allow such a vile animal near his child. His skin crawled at the thought of him touching her, and he knew he was lost. His swollen face and broken limbs were nothing compared to the anguish he felt for his daughter.

"I can't let that devil touch you, Rosie. I'd rather die than let that happen to my little girl. Listen now, you *can't* save me. I want you to get on your horse and ride away. *Please*." Old Reilly grasped his daughter's shoulders and shook her, desperate to make her see sense, but she was adamant.

"I must do this, because I don't want you to die. I won't ride away… I have no choice."

Rosa passed the gallows as she returned to Judge Mather. As the ropes quivered in the gentle wind, and the timbers creaked, she stopped for a moment, unable to move her eyes, until her reverie was broken by the baying of a hound close by. She quickened her step, and with a heavy heart continued on her path. Later that night, she would pay a price for her father's life.

V. Seven Curses on a Judge So Cruel.

The sun shone brightly through the curtains as Rosa awoke the next morning. The settee on which she had rested had inflicted all sorts of aches upon her body, which was barely covered. But it was over. She sat up, enraptured by the tranquil silence of the morning. A perfect morning. Then, just faintly, she heard a sound which froze every drop of blood within her body. Closing her eyes, she forced herself to stand and walk toward the open window, where she was able to see within the courtyard the hanging, broken body of her father. Holding her hand to her mouth, she cried out, as she realised what had happened. The judge had had no intention of freeing her father. He just wanted the pleasure of torturing him as much as possible, knowing Old Reilly wouldn't have been able to bear having his daughter corrupted. She could have spent her father's last hours by his side, but Judge Mather had stolen her away.

Her body began to burn with the rage she now felt. She threw on her clothes, which were scattered across the floor, and ran through the building, imploring people to tell her of the judge's whereabouts. In the saloon down on Twelfth Street, they told her. She ran as fast as she could, not daring to meet her father's deadened eyes in the courtyard. She found her destination and barged through its doors. Inside, the conversation cut off and all eyes fell on the panting black girl, whose expression was one of utter hatred. As Rosa descended upon Montgomery's celebrated judge, he tilted his head upwards with a look of satisfaction, until she raised her finger accusingly and chanted, so that every man could hear,

>"These be seven curses on a judge so cruel:
>"That one doctor will not save him,
>"That two healers will not heal him,
>"That three eyes will not see him.
>"That four ears will not hear him,
>"That five walls will not hide him,
>"That six diggers will not bury him
>"And that seven deaths shall never kill him."

A transposition of the Bob Dylan song Seven Curses.

WATCHING THE LAST SMOKE

Paul Clayton

In our city, the great historic capital of this Siberian hinterland, the two tallest buildings stand side by side as vast twin monuments to our country's haltered progress from archaic to modern. My office in the concrete monstrosity of the Finance Tower (the taller of the pair) overlooks, with a clear view of the roof, the adjacent University Tower. At those times when a person can simply no longer bear to trudge through the filthy bog of paperwork, studying strangers' bank accounts looking for discrepancies for which the bank can recover the smallest amounts of hard-fiddled cash, the view from my desk is a welcome distraction. One such distraction came in January last, on the coldest day of a terrible winter.

The University Tower is an enormous gothic masterpiece, with high stained glass windows, parapets and gargoyles, a dark but beautiful reminder of a time when architecture was more important than people. A large, flat section of the roof provided sanctuary for many an academic on his cigarette break. Over time, in my role as voyeur at my banker's desk, I came to know the faces of the characters in my rooftop soap opera. Despite its status as capital, our city is a small one, and for those who want to know people, knowing people is easy. And so my characters' faces eventually had names and histories, habits and inclinations and some days I spent more time watching the activity on the roof top than I did scrutinizing suspicious bank accounts.

On this day Professor Tomas Marasyk, revered historian and collector of renaissance paintings, stood at the edge of the roof facing westward. It was one of those days where you can literally smell the cold and the northerly wind was causing the weathervane to spin so fast that I could barely see it. It was not snowing at this moment, but the previous night's fall had been heavy and there was a thick blanket on the ground. Marasyk had been standing on the roof all morning and was blowing into his leather-clad hands and rubbing them together intermittently. It was the day after the new parliament had been sworn into office and Marasyk had reason to be concerned. Rumour was rife that he had collaborated with the previous government on a number of shadowy and sinister projects involving historic analysis of oppressive aristocratic regimes. I was sceptical of these allegations to say the least. If nothing else, it seemed like a clichéd and cartoon-like sketch of a bad government being naughty. Whether Marasyk had been involved with the party at all was pure speculation, although his right-leaning tendencies were there to be seen. Nevertheless, the new socially democratic government had come to power with a narrow margin of votes that appeared to rely heavily on their insistence that these dark rumours were hard facts and that it meant disaster for the working classes. Considering the ratio of working class people in this poverty-addled country of ours, I suspect they had presumed a much more resounding victory. In order to save face and concrete over their exaggerations, a number of the alleged chief perpetrators had been swiftly rounded up and brought into

36

custody. In hindsight, I believe Marasyk knew he was going to be arrested that day and he considered that the rooftop of the University Tower was as good a place as any to spend his last few hours of liberty.

Monika, the filing clerk, brought my morning coffee, black and bitter, just as Karel, the university's janitor, stepped out onto the roof. Marasyk turned and nodded his greeting to Karel. The pair were familiar to each other and had often spent time together in silence smoking into the winter air. We are a nation of smokers. Something struck me as odd about the little rendezvous on the rooftop that day. On every other occasion that Marasyk and Karel have smoked together in my window-show, they have never once shared cigarettes. Marasyk preferred his expensive, hand-rolled Italian cigarillos, and preferred not to hand them around. The janitor smoked, probably through necessity, the rough, cheap, factory produced, local filterless brand. Today, for reasons that I am never likely to discern, when Karel proffered his paper pack in Marasyk's direction, the professor chose to take one. I watched with interest, sipping thick black liquid from the cheap company-emblazoned porcelain. Marasyk's first drag caused a small wrench that went unnoticed by his companion. After that he settled into sucking away at that little stick of heavenly poison, despite it probably tearing his delicate throat to shreds. Even now, not a word had passed between them.

After the cigarettes were smoked, the janitor turned to return to his work but in direct breach of the code between these two men of silence, Marasyk called him back. He asked a question. I imagined that he was enquiring of the health of Karel's eldest son, who had been ill. The janitor's shoulder's slumped, he looked at his feet and shook his head. The boy had died the day before. The professor's arm rested instinctively on the shoulder of the younger man. He gestured an exaggerated shrug which I took to be an incredulous query as to why the man was working if his son had just died. Karel looked him angrily in the eye. He had to feed his family. Nobody was going to pay him for not doing his job. Marasyk's arm fell to his side. He shook his head solemnly and reached inside his jacket for his cigarillo case. The janitor politely refused his hand-rolled, vanilla-papered offer and instead lit up one of his own ragged cigarettes. They returned to their positions gazing westward and smoked, once more in silence as the snow began to fall.

The janitor returned to work and Professor Marasyk paced up and down in the falling snow until lunchtime. I returned with my stew from the staff kitchen to eat at my desk, as I often did when there was somebody to watch on the roof, perplexed at the academic's blasé attitude towards the weather. He sat on his haunches leaning against a wall, hugging himself for warmth. His determination to stay outside was impressive, but I began to feel a little concerned. Nobody should expose themselves to the elements in this desperate, bitter, wintry city for longer than they must. I wondered if he would turn blue. The phone rang.

"Hello."

"Have you noticed Marasyk?" It was Petr from the office down the hall.

"I've been watching him all morning."

"Did you see he smoked one of Karel's cigarettes?"

"Yes, he's never done that before."

"No he did once," Petr said. He was more of a studious chronicler of events than I. "It was a few months ago, but I think he only took it then because there was somebody else on the roof and he didn't want to share his cigarillos."

"You're a cynic Petr."

"Say, how do you fancy clubbing together and investing in some art?"

"What are you talking about?"

"I've heard there will be some very old paintings going cheap. Art never depreciates in value."

"What do you know about paintings?" I usually wanted no part of Petr's crazy money-making ventures, but I liked art and curiosity caused me to bite.

"I know nothing about art at all. But I do have it on good authority that some of Marasyk's collection will be going on sale on the cheap."

"Why would he sell? He's been building that collection for years."

"He wouldn't sell. But here's the thing, he's broke. That's why he's been standing out there all morning. He can't afford his legal fees. I've no doubt whatsoever that Professor Art-Critic over there is mulling over his dark future in gaol. His precious collection would easily pay for his costs, and I heard from Leah on the third floor, whose aunt cleans for the family, that his wife would sell with or without his consent."

"Even if this two-bit rumour is true, how do you suppose we could afford even one piece of that collection?" Petr's ideas were mostly hair-brained, but this one was worse than usual.

"I have one word for you my sceptical friend…" He paused, as if to add an unlikely amount of drama to his ridiculous proposal. "Consortium."

I groaned and hung up the telephone. How he thought a group of poorly paid bank clerks were going to club together and buy an art collection, I have no idea. I mopped up the remaining gravy from my bowl of stew with a chunk of bread.

Then I noticed a group of new figures on the rooftop. I didn't recognize any of them, but two of them were in the military-cum-police uniform of an agency unfamiliar to me. The third was a small man with spectacles and a red scarf. After the fact, the newspaper reports, and the official report, which I took the trouble of looking up in the state library, all claimed that Marasyk had died from a single gunshot wound to the head. The marksman responded, the reports held, to the professor 'wielding a shining object' which turned out to be his cigarillo case. Now neither Petr nor I consider these to be the facts. What we both saw was Marasyk with both hands firmly planted in his outside pockets as he turned to face the men. We know from observation that he keeps his silver case in his inside pocket. As Marasyk took a step forward, no doubt to allow himself to be put under arrest, the uniformed men drew their handguns and fired repeatedly into his torso. The only bullet I saw go in his head was when his thoroughly dead, punctured body lay pouring brilliant red into the snow and the small man with the glasses took a gun and shot him point blank in the face.

It always puzzled me how the investigators managed to side-step the autopsy, but I suppose that tells its own tale. Mrs Marasyk sold the whole collection to a museum in London for a princely sum and disappeared. When I think back on that day, the thing that always upsets me the most is the thought of Karel, having shared that cigarette only hours before, having to clean up the mess left by his companion's murdered corpse.

Oliver Janson

The car pulled up to the kerb. I opened the front door to find an old green telephone sat in the passenger seat.

"What's that for?" I asked.

Mum looked over at me and said, "Just get in the back."

"Where are we going?"

She eyed me in the mirror and said, "You'll see when we get there."

Last week I'd come home from a party I wasn't supposed to be at, covered in sick and crying my eyes out. I couldn't see well enough to open the front door and slip in quietly like I planned on the walk home. My fumbling woke Mum up. She asked me what was wrong.

"Jason," I replied. He was two years above me in school and I'd been obsessed with him for as long as I could remember. I'd had too much to drink and decided to tell him how I felt, only for him to turn me down.

"What about him?" she demanded.

I don't remember exactly what I said next, I think I blacked out for a minute or two, but somehow I gave her the impression that he'd forced himself on me.

"Oh baby," she said throwing her arms around me. "Don't worry."

I was so confused, I didn't know what I'd just said, and I couldn't remember the last time Mum held me like that. It felt so good in her arms. I began to cry again.

"It'll be okay," she continued, holding me close. "I'll make it all better, don't you worry."

It's stupid, but I liked her attention. If I told her the truth it would just push her even further away than before. I was sure I'd get to telling her the truth one day. Maybe after I'd left home.

It was getting dark outside. I looked out as the moon flickered through the trees. The car slowed down, then stopped. We were at the back of a line; I could see blue lights flashing up ahead.

"What's happened?" I asked.

"Looks like an accident or something," Mum replied. A policeman walked up to the car in front and spoke to the driver for a few moments, before standing back to let the car pull out and drive past the waiting cars towards the flashing lights ahead.

I checked my seatbelt was done up.

"Good evening ma'am," the policeman said as he reached our car.

"Evening officer," Mum replied.

.

"There's been an accident up ahead. These drivers," he gestured to those in front, "are waiting to give statements. We needn't detain you. The road is open on the right – the officer down there will wave you through when your way is clear. Please drive carefully."

"Okay, thank you," said Mum. The policeman nodded and stood back from the window. Mum pulled away slowly and drove up beyond the waiting line. The people in their cars looked freaked out. One woman sat alone crying. Another man was talking into his mobile, his face pale and blank. A second policeman signalled for us to drive on.

I looked out to see what had happened. Over on the left side of the road a small red car was bent around a tree. Bright green and yellow jackets huddled together by the car, and one of them moved away towards the ambulance. Through flickers of blue I saw a body. A shapeless mess of blood and shattered bone where there should have been a face. It mouthed toothlessly at those standing over it, but they couldn't hear what it said or chose to ignore it.

Feeling sick I checked my seatbelt again. The car moved back to the left as we passed the last police car.

"Can you put the radio on please Mum?" I said – anything to take my mind off of that face.

"All right," Mum said reaching down to turn on the radio.

We continued down the same road for some time. I sat trying to forget the accident, but the image was burned into my mind. Eventually, in the middle of nowhere, Mum pulled into a lay-by at the side of the road.

"We're here," she chirped.

"We are? Where?" I asked.

Mum picked the phone up from the seat next to her. "Come on," she said looking round at me, "it's only a little walk now."

"To what?" I was beginning to get pissed off with all this secrecy.

"You'll never find out if you just sit here," she said stepping out of the car.

"I guess so," I replied.

I followed Mum as she headed down a path through the trees. Walking behind her I began to feel guilty. Maybe something had snapped in her mind because of me.

"What's the phone for then?" I asked.

She kept on walking ahead. Without looking back she replied, "You wouldn't believe me if I told you. You've got to see it."

As we walked I noticed that amongst the trees houses were beginning to appear. They were falling apart, windows missing or broken, and any doors remaining rotting away. It was hard to tell if anyone had ever lived here.

"What is this place?" I asked.

"This is where I grew up," Mum said.

"What happened?"

"Oh, you know, people move away," she said as if it explained why an entire village had been deserted and left to rot. Before I could ask anything else Mum veered off towards the back of one house. "This is it," she said as she walked into what used to be the back garden. She stopped at the bottom of the garden by a big tree stump. She took the phone from under her arm and placed it on the stump. Too confused to speak, I watched her kneel down and brush some leaves away before scratching a hole in the dirt beneath. "Okay," she muttered, taking the end of the phone line and placing it into the opening. She rose to her feet. Nothing happened. I was sure her mind was gone, this didn't make any sense.

Suddenly the line sparked and a buzzing sound seemed to fill the forest. The phone started ringing. It was an old ring, the sound of metal hitting metal. I looked over at Mum. She picked up the receiver with a trembling hand.

"Hello, are you there?" she asked.

I moved closer to try and hear whoever she was speaking to; I could hear something but not enough to tell if it was a real voice. She stood silent for a moment. Her eyes stared out straight in front of her but she didn't seem to be focused on anything. She spoke into the phone. "I need you to do something for me."

A man's distorted laugh crackled loudly through the ear piece.

Mum held the phone away from her ear for moment before continuing, "Jason Howell. H-O-W-E-L-L. Got it? Born January 21st 1988. Is that enough?" A second passed before Mum said, "Good." There was a burst of static as the connection died. Mum jerked the receiver away from her ear and placed it back on the phone. The buzzing was gone.

She knelt down, pulled the line out of the ground and wrapped it around the phone. She stood back up. I looked at her eyes, still fixed on nothing and now welling up.

"What the hell is going on?" I asked.

No reply.

I waved my hands in front of her and shouted, "Hey!"

Her eyes snapped onto me, full of confusion. She looked like she had just woken up from a sleep she didn't know she had fallen into. "What?" she asked.

"Jason, Mum. What's going to happen to him?"

The confusion fell from her eyes as she calmly replied, "Oh, he's dead now sweetheart." She began walking away from the tree stump, back towards the front of the house.

Following her closely I said, "That's not funny, what's really going to happen?"

Mum continued her way past the house. "He's dead, dear," she said.

I grabbed her by the shoulder and pulled her round to face me. "What the fuck are you on about? How is he dead? Who were you speaking to?"

"The next time he goes to sleep he won't wake up." Mum wiped her nose with the back of her free hand. "That's how it works, and that's all I know."

"We can't kill him," I explained.

"We won't."

I looked at her to try and work out if she realised exactly what she was saying, but she wasn't confused anymore.

"But we're responsible," I said.

Anger flashed into her eyes. "He's responsible," she shouted. "He brought this on himself, not you and not me. Isn't this what you wanted?"

"No! No, Mum, this isn't what I wanted," I shouted back at her. "I don't know what I told you, but it was a lie. Nothing happened. I wanted it to but he turned me down. He turned me down Mum. That's why I was crying. But if I'd told you that you'd have just gone on ignoring me, like before."

Mum looked hurt and confused. "What are you talking about? You said he hurt you. If this isn't what you wanted then why didn't you stop me?" she asked.

"How could I stop you when I had no idea what you were doing? You didn't tell me anything. I asked you what the phone was for and you ignored me."

"You said he hurt you. I only did it because I love you. I'm sorry, I'm so sorry." She reached out to hold me, I pushed her back.

"Can we stop it?" I asked.

"No," Mum said, "it's too late now."

That was it, there was no point shouting anymore. I couldn't forgive her. Not ever. I started back toward the car.

"Let's go," I said. We walked in silence. There was nothing left to say.

Princess Anorexia

An hourglass she
used to be,
now
a skeleton surfacing
through passing storms of broken sands
fighting for the time
to free
the bony belle with shaky hands.

Through the Looking Glass

I see life upside down, in frames
when the angle of the glass is right;
walk into walls without pain.
I see life upside down, in frames.
I blame old boring childhood games
for being charmed by the light
and for seeing life upside down in frames –
when the angle of the glass is right.

Carley Moulton

44

Splinter

I pick a loose piece of skin
around the thumb,
nibble it away.
I don't want to walk past,
might fall over,
spill my drink,
a pain that can niggle
for weeks
until it is lost
under threads of flesh.

Sweat drips down
the pearls of my spine.
I crouch against
vibrating walls,
the seventies bubble glass
feels cool,
as my feet cradle the vodka.
I watch your jacket
working the room,
memories of nights leaving early,
for tea and toast.

I casually suck
a slice of lemon,
push my tongue
through panels of bitter tissue,
pretending I haven't
noticed *you* stroking the arm
of *her* all swinging hips
and clicking heels.

I used to love this place,
drinking until
I could no longer taste
the endless cigarettes.
I stand as if to leave, but
a fragment of wood
once dug in
travels through the body,
working its way,
poisoning the blood.

Gemma Kenyon

FAB RED VINTAGE TEA DRESS 1940S L@@K

Katie Popperwell

Beautiful red 100% silk tea dress with gold ginkgo leaf pattern. Reasonable vintage condition. Slightly frayed at the hem and with some wear at back of skirt.

The single, blurry photo showed a dressmaker's dummy, her stiff headless body covered with a garish paisley, standing against a bare brick wall. The dress draped over her frame belonged at a garden party with a curled head and perfect décolleté. Beatrice could offer it no such thing. She didn't go to parties, she didn't wear dresses, and her dark hair was too short to curl. Her fingers moved as she imagined touching the aged silk, the softness and perfect thickness of it, the smell of mothballs and attics. Forgotten places. She spent some minutes telling herself that she would let it go, that she didn't need it, that it was impractical, but even as she did so her excitement was mounting. This token denial was all part of the ritual. Four bids already. Two days, four hours, 38 minutes until end of auction. 6.37am Sunday morning. The chosen moniker of the current high bidder was scotslass77.

Beatrice wondered what kind of girl would wear a dress like this. What kind of girl would want it so much that she had already placed a bid so early in the game? She couldn't help imagining a slim girl in her early twenties; pretty, blonde, the kind of girl that might go to parties in the dress, have a job, maybe even a career, the kind of girl that could laugh easily with boys, safe in the knowledge that she was charming, but not too flirtatious. It wasn't that kind of dress. She had a steady boyfriend, but they wouldn't live together, she was too independent, and so young, why would she want to be tied down so early? No, perhaps she was even thinking of breaking up with him, perhaps that's why she wanted the dress, to wear on her first night out with the girls, her friends, they would be so pleased that she was single again, you know what these girls are like…

The front door opened, Beatrice closed the browser window, shut down the computer and went into the kitchen.

6 bids: 1d 2h 48m.

Two more bids and scotslass77 still the high bidder. Beatrice glanced around the room at the remains of tonight's meal sitting on the coffee table. An empty can of coke had fallen on the floor, leaked the last of its gluey juice onto the carpet and stuck together the pages of her magazine. The static brightness of the screen drew back her gaze. The dress was even more beautiful than she remembered. The colour looked richer than before, the fabric tumbled around legless air in ripples and waves worthy of classic sculpture, the hypnotic geometry of the pattern was alive with the gentle pulsing of the computer. She scrolled down to the bottom of the page.

Q: Is there any size info on label? If not could you
measure waist pls?
A: Waist measures 26in. flat. Label faded.

Scotslass77 would have a 26in waist. She didn't have curves, she was tall and willowy, some people probably said that she was too thin but people always say that about slim girls, say they're too thin then splash them all over the magazines. She'd probably lost weight too because of the boyfriend; all her friends would be saying she looked great. She'd smile and thank them but it wouldn't go to her head because she'd got that sort of self-assurance where it didn't seem to matter what she looked like. It did matter though, Beatrice knew that. This girl loved it, you just knew she did. She could wear whatever she wanted and look fabulous, and she wanted this dress, but she wasn't going to get it. The dress belonged to Beatrice, and no skinny Scottish bitch was going to take it away from her. Clicking the 'place bid' button she set her maximum bid at a price higher than she could afford. An uneven number, so that scotslass77 would never guess it. Her breath was still while the system digested her request, her eyes dry and prickling, her heart beating hard, alive and fierce.

You are the current high bidder.

Beatrice touched the floor with her big toe and began to twirl on the battered office chair until she was pirouetting wildly, her eyes fixed on the screen. She whipped her head round again and again, always finding her mark, while the rest of the room became a blur.

Spent, Beatrice turned off the computer. The empty screen became a mirror and she turned away. Looking down at the elasticated waistband of her pyjama bottoms she pushed her index finger sharply into the almost visible bump that was beginning to emerge from the folds of flesh around her middle and felt the hardness there that would not go away. She moved her fingers around her waist then along her arms, hugging herself, digging her nails into the flesh.

Pulling her thick towelling dressing gown around herself she went upstairs and got into bed, tensing her abdomen and willing gravity to pull in her tummy as she lay on her back.

He rolled over and slipped his arm around her.

That night she dreamt of a slim girl with long legs and moonlight in her hair. She was dancing, drinking and wearing a red silk dress, and laughing, laughing at her. She woke up alone, sweating, in too many layers and feeling sick. In the bathroom she stuck her fingers down her throat and felt better.

Letting her rank, heavy clothes fall on the floor; she stepped into the shower and closed her eyes as the hot water streamed over her body. Lost in steam, she cradled the memory of the red dress and the woman who would never have it. Scotslass77 would be naked, cold, would have to wear a cheap modern dress made of synthetic fabric while Beatrice would be effortlessly chic and alluring in her one-of-a-kind vintage treasure. The silk would slip over her thighs and belly like hot liquid, melting away all her imperfections to reveal the true Beatrice. Witty, confident and sexy, she could be all these things if only she had the right chance, the right life, the right dress.

She opened her eyes, turned off the shower and watched the steam condense on the cold window, trickle down and form a dirty puddle in the grouting.

9 bids: 12m

The sky was still dark when she made her way downstairs on Sunday morning. Sitting at her computer in those last minutes, Beatrice could almost feel the other girl, sitting at her own computer, planning, calculating, looking at the same image on a different screen. It was all there to be decided: whose desire was the strongest, who was the cleverest, the quickest, the most deserving of the prize. The screen remained static, except for the changing digits tracking the move toward zero hour. Beatrice, taut and awake, kept her eyes fixed and with four minutes to go was seized with panic. What if *she* was waiting right until the last minute? What if she had guessed at her highest bid? It suddenly didn't seem such a clever number after all. Beatrice bid against herself again and again and again, the number of bids changed from 10, to 11, to 12, with no other activity. Then it was over.

Congratulations, you won the item!

She gave the air a small victory punch, shut down the browser and went to make a cup of tea.

The dress arrived on a Tuesday morning, wrapped in a plastic bag inside a reused brown paper envelope. Beatrice tore open the parcel joyfully. It was frayed in more places than the seller had admitted and the colour was a dark orange that reminded Beatrice of the upholstery on her grandmother's couch. She picked up the shreds of paper and plastic from the floor and, cradling them gently in her arms, carried the desecrated remains of the parcel upstairs. She hung the dress in her wardrobe on a grey plastic hanger. Leaving the wardrobe door open and sitting on the end of the bed she surveyed the row of tattered dresses hanging before her. The light from the window illuminated dusty rainbows of faded pinks, reds and greens in silk, taffeta and cotton, a phantom chorus line of unlived lives, empty husks, no less cruel for their stillness. Beatrice pulled her arms tight around her body and lay down on the bed, soaking the sheets with her tears.

ALWAYS THE HERO

Christopher Myers

The newspaper slides through the door. Kevin picks it up and sees himself staring back with his arms around two kids, all of them smiling idiotically. 'Local Hero Saves Children,' the headline reads. Certainly not the most original headline, he thinks, or the most accurate. He considers reading it but is interrupted by the phone.

'Hello.'

'Oh my God.'

'Hi mum.'

'Why didn't you tell me?' she yells.

'It isn't a big deal.'

'You run in to a burning house and that's not a big deal?'

'I was going to tell you.'

'Well you might not have got chance. What if you'd passed out from the smoke or what if the roof had collapsed?'

'Someone had to help.'

'The people that are supposed to help ride around in big red trucks and get paid to do it, you damn fool. Why do you always have to be the hero?'

'I don't know.'

He manages to cut her short and puts the phone down. He picks up the newspaper, dumps it in the bin then heads for work. He's dreading the office. Another day of praise awaits him. Nausea lurks inside his stomach as he prays for a quiet day.

He's barely through the door when Amy greets him.

'Good morning Mr Wight.'

'Morning Amy.'

'How are you today?'

'I'm fine thank you. Thought I'd make an early start.' He walks quickly past her to his desk. He's surprised she didn't mention it. He was certain she would. Maybe she hasn't heard? He sits down and begins to organise his paperwork. When he looks up she's there again.

'Can I just say…'

'Yes?'

'That what you did,' a pause, 'was,' another pause, 'amazing!' Her face is beaming. 'If only there were more men out there like you. To think that you risked your own life for children you didn't even know!'

He doesn't know what to say. It doesn't seem that she does either. She just stands there with a smile that keeps on growing, her eyes fixed on him.

Eventually he responds. 'I'm sure anyone would have done the same.'

'But they wouldn't,' she counters excitedly. 'You're one in a million. If only there were more men like you.' She's repeating herself now. Twirling her hair around her fingers is already enough indication of her stupidity, he thinks, but it's the fact that she follows him around with puppy dog eyes every time he does something like this that truly results in him granting her the title of 'Idiot.' Yet he can't rid himself of the thought that he could probably sleep with her if he tried it on.

'Would you like to go out Saturday night?' he asks.

Her smile somehow gets even bigger. 'Sure!' She almost skips back to her desk. He's surprised she finds her way.

Girls love heroes. That's why Amy obsesses over him. Kevin knows guys who waste their wages on flowers, meals, chocolate, jewellery and within a week they're dumped. But if you run in to a burning house and throw two kids out of the back door you're irresistible.

For the next hour or so, Kevin is congratulated by just about every member of the office. His worshippers use words such as 'hero,' 'brave,' 'courageous,' and so on. He tries to ignore them. His mind isn't on their compliments, it's on his own actions. What if he hadn't have saved those kids? What if he'd just left their little bodies to burn? He sees two tiny charred corpses in his head. A sickly image, but not one that upsets him. A fact that disturbs him.

On his way to the coffee machine he sees Jamie walking towards him. Jamie angers him but he can't avoid him now; eye contact has been made.

'Hello there Kevin,' he booms.

'All right mate?'

'Don't know if you've heard,' he whips out a form, 'but next weekend I'm doing some charity work for AFKCIA – that's Alliance For Kids Coping In Africa to you and me buddy.' He winks. 'Don't know if you've heard of them but they're a fantastic new little organisation that's trying to help African kids.' His face all of a sudden adopts a sad look. 'Those poor little blighters over there are having a heck of a hard time. So it's up to guys like you and me to help them out and get them on their feet.' The smile's back. 'So what do you say Kev? I'm doing a sponsored run while dressed as a kangaroo to hopefully raise a few hundred quid.'

'Sounds great.'

'Fancy sponsoring me mate?'

'Sure thing, count me in.'

Kevin signs the form, donates £3.54 a mile (topping the previous top sponsor by four pence) and Jamie's off on his way. He despises Jamie. He knew Jamie wouldn't be able to do it – wouldn't be able to congratulate him. Jamie must have known but as usual he was too busy with his own affairs. Kevin knows what this charity thing is about; it's about upstaging him. He wonders what posseses a man to dress up as a kangaroo and knacker themselves out in some dumb charity run. Because he's a good guy who wants to help the less fortunate? Hell no, Kevin thinks, he's just after applause … but what about Kevin?

Why did he risk his own life to save two children he didn't even know? Was it because he cared? He can't answer that.

He tries to forget about it. It's not the first time he's questioned his own actions. Lately he's been concerned about his motives. Does he genuinely want to be a good guy or is it because he's scared of being found out? Jamie probably knows. In some ways they're alike, both do-gooders. Except Kevin does it with style. Jamie goes on fun runs, buys cheap nasty clothes from charity shops and other lame stuff. Kevin's good deeds are dramatic. They could base a film on his actions. He imagines a slow motion shot of himself running out of the blaze, a kid under each arm, diving out the door and on to the grass as the house explodes behind him. While the house hadn't actually exploded he wishes it had; that would have been cool.

Unlike Kevin, Jamie doesn't get the glory. He gets the odd compliment, sometimes even a pat on the back. But he doesn't get the girls or the newspaper headlines. He's not going out with the office babe on Saturday. He's spending his Saturday boiling to death in a kangaroo costume with only the smell of his own perspiration for company. Kevin wins. But it feels tainted. It feels fake.

Someone smacks him on the shoulder.

'Hey Big Man.' It's Mike. 'Fancy a few drinks with the lads at The Crown later?'

'Don't see why not.'

'Good lad, good lad. You sure it won't interfere with your superhero commitments though?' Mike laughs loudly. 'I'm just yanking your chain. See you later mate.'

That should help. Drink always helps. If he drinks enough his conscience will be buried under talk of birds, football and asylum seekers. Rob always brings asylum seekers up. He blames them for everything. Kevin and Mike usually stand up for them. Why does he stand up for them though? Does he really care? Does he really...? He's doing it again.

The rest of the day at work passes in much the same way. People who've already congratulated him do so again, prying for more details of his heroic actions. By the time five o'clock comes around he's exhausted. He walks in to The Crown. All eyes are on him. His mates greet him. After a few minutes they sense he's not willing to divulge any more details on his adventure in the burning house. The talk goes back to the usual.

'I saw you talking to that blonde Amy at work,' Rob says with a wink.

Mike interrupts: 'Which Amy is that?'

'Blonde busty Amy.'

'Whoa, blonde busty Amy, eh? Anything going on there son?'

'There better be. I wouldn't mind giving her a good seeing to myself,' Rob says with another wink.

'Oh yes. All the way to the bank,' Mike booms.

Kevin laughs it off. He doesn't say anything about his upcoming date. Unlike his heroics his conquests are kept secret. He never shows off about his ladies. That must be a good side to his personality, he thinks. He doesn't kiss and tell out of respect … and partly because if his antics were made public it could ruin future conquests.

Mike can sense his troubles. 'What's been up with you today?'

'Nothing, I'm fine.'

'You've done nothing but mope around all day. You're the local hero – you should be on top of the world.'

'I'm fine.'

'Girlfriend dumped you?'

'I don't have a girlfriend.'

'A-ha, so that's it. You're lonely.'

'I'm not bothered about having a girlfriend.'

'Not bothered? There's something wrong with you mate.'

Once Mike gets going he doesn't shut up. Kevin knows Mike's trying to do his best but that doesn't make him any less annoying.

'Well what's wrong?'

'Nothing.'

'Someone died?'

'No.'

'Even if they had you wouldn't tell me, would you? You need to express yourself more lad. Be more vocal.'

'Whatever.'

'You sure no one's died?'

Kevin can't be doing with this. He looks at his friends. Idiots! Vulgar and predictable. All of their body gestures during conversation seem to involve either thrusting or something else disgustingly explicit. Yet behind their crass conversations lie morals. They look out for each other. If they sense he's having trouble they're always there. He envies these traits.

A few months ago Mike had a cancer scare. That night had been the first in a long time that he'd seen grown men cry. While the rest of them worried about their mate, Kevin fantasised about what this situation would bring him. He imagined telling some beautiful girl about his heartbreak and her being astonished by the empathy that he possessed. He had a moving speech planned out for the funeral. Disappointingly for Kevin the speech ended up being of no use as Mike was given the all clear.

'What's wrong with me?' he mutters to himself.

He leaves the pub early. The rest of them will be there till late but he wants to be on his own. His thoughts return to analysing his own actions. Maybe he needs to see a psychiatrist.

He hears a scream. It's coming from down a small street. He sees an old woman trying to fend off a man. Kevin starts to run. 'Local Hero Strikes Again,' a headline reads in his head. He stops. He doesn't want that. The man's running towards him now with the old woman's bag. Kevin's bigger than the mugger, he can stop him.

Kevin doesn't.

He steps out of the man's way and he's off in to the night.

'Why didn't you stop him?' the woman shrieks. Kevin doesn't answer. He doesn't owe her or anyone anything. He's had enough of this. He begins to walk away when he hears another scream. Kevin turns around to see her falling to the floor, clutching her chest. He didn't expect this. He walks towards her and sees her face twisting in agony. Her body's shaking, arms grasping at thin air. Then he feels it. It hits him hard. Guilt. Real guilt. A real emotional response to someone else's pain. She continues to gasp. He could have stopped this. The guilt won't shift. The feeling of empathy is completely new to him and it's crippling. Then he realises… He does care. This woman's pain has caused a genuine sense of anguish in him. He feels her pain.

'I'm human!' He starts to laugh. The empathy fades away as possibilities of the man he can now be run through his mind. As he watches the old woman gasping for breath, he smiles. He truly is a good guy.

Dream of Hollow Sigh

Demons on my pillow
Diamonds in my mind,
Fingers weaved from willow
And in your darkness find
Memories full of silver,
Shadows full of light,
A cup of love to fill her
Then bind the willow tight.

Tongue of honey whispers
Cradled in my eye
Making love's resistor
In the Dream of Hollow Sigh.
Finger on the pulse of hell
Hollow, deep and sweet
Confessions harlot's heart will sell,
To seal her will's defeat.

Drowning in the river
Falling in the flood,
Touch that lets me shiver
Clawing at the mud,
Flaxen hair and golden heart
Brushing at my skin,
Blood red wine and strawberry tart
And the sweeter taste of sin.

Hum of treble healing
Dealt behind the throng,
Soft in tender feeling
Shared in bitter song.
Tidal rhythm climbing,
Heavy, strong and low,
Attuned to pagan timing
Buried in the flow.

Stuart Cannell

LOVE AND TEMPTATION

John Holding

The local paper sat on the waiting room table, its headline to the fore. Alec didn't need to pick it up; he recalled the fuss at the time and the buzz that had overtaken the town. The memory was a welcome distraction, a reminder of happier times. The Laird, a balding middle-aged bachelor, seemingly destined to remain single all his days, had won the heart of a dark, dazzling young beauty. The whole town was swept along in wedding fervour for its landowner and first citizen. For weeks the place had shone whilst dressed in all its finery. The streets bedecked in flags and bunting, an abundance of colourful celebration. The decorations were a clever merging of Ullemere's historic past with its business and tourist centre aspirations. Hundreds had lined the streets outside the Kirk to cheer the happy couple, Eileen and Fiona among them. In truth, the Town Councillors had pulled off a marketing masterstroke. The 300 year-old Ullemere Ring, once a gift from the first Laird of Ullemere to his wife, had languished in the Town Hall display case gathering dust. In gifting it back to the current Laird for his young bride, the Council generated media interest and publicity far in excess of the ring's undoubted value. Yet now, less than 12 months on, the papers proclaimed the fairytale at an end. The Laird's beautiful wife was dead, the victim of a horse riding accident. The Laird had shut himself away, inconsolable with grief and the town was immersed in misery; Alec could identify with that.

Alec sat with his hands in his lap and stared at the wall opposite, lest he catch someone's eye. *It's bad enough to be seen in here; I don't want people discussing my business; and I don't need their pity.* His hands played his baseball cap through his fingers until he realised he was wringing the life from it and pulled them apart so quickly he almost dropped the cap. *God, I hope no-one noticed, or they'll have me on the verge of a breakdown.*

The nursing administrator announced the next appointment, "Alec Thomson, please."

He stood; she smiled at him. She was pretty and he knew the smile was intended to put him at ease, yet he couldn't bring himself to return it.

"Dr Cooper will see you now."

The young doctor was flicking through Alec's medical notes. "Take a seat, Mr Thomson. It's been four weeks since your last appointment, how have you been holding up?"

"Okay, I suppose, Doctor."

"Has your wife been in touch at all?"

"She contacted some neighbours to say that she and Fiona were fine. Said she'll make arrangements for me to see Fiona in due course but that she needs space for a while, whatever that means."

"And how do you feel about that?"

"How would you feel about your neighbours knowing your business?" Alec paused, relaxing his grip on the twisted baseball cap. "I'm sorry, I didn't mean that to come out the way it did."

"That's okay. It's natural that you feel a little defensive. How were the pills I prescribed for you – have they helped?"

"They did, but I'm sleeping better these days. I can do without them now."

"Okay, but let's just give you a once-over, just to be sure." The doctor checked Alec's blood pressure, then his eyes and the inside of his mouth. He listened to his chest and finally looked at his fingernails. "Are you eating properly?"

"I miss Eileen's cooking, but I'm getting by."

"Just make sure you vary your diet." He sat back in his seat and bit his lower lip before continuing. "You're in fine shape physically, Alec. Indeed, I'd be happy to have your physique myself at 40, but let me rephrase that earlier question. Have you accepted your marital situation?"

Alec shifted in his seat and folded his arms, though he still clung to his cap. "I've accepted that Eileen has left me. But that doesn't mean I'm happy about it or that I don't want her back."

The doctor pushed his chair back from the desk. "I can see that you're still hurting, and that's perfectly understandable. But we don't want you falling prey to depression. Try not to dwell on things. Find something positive to aim for and concentrate on achieving it, bit by bit if need be. Give Eileen the time and space she needs and if it's right, maybe you'll get back together. If not … well, then you'll be emotionally strong enough to move on."

Alec nodded. "If I'm honest, it wasn't quite as unexpected as I've made out. Eileen and I had occasional arguments over money. She felt I lacked ambition and drive, she was tired of us scraping by on a gravedigger's wage."

Dr Cooper looked puzzled. "But it says in the file that you work for the Council Parks and Gardens. Doesn't that mean you get involved in all sorts of things?"

"Sure, most days I'm a gardener but I've had formal training. if there's a burial then it's me who digs the grave. Say it once and it's all folks remember, so she's got a point. I amount to no more than a gravedigger."

"So you'll play a major role in tomorrow's funeral then?"

"If you can call digging a hole then filling it in again a major role then, yes. Was it you who found her, Doctor?"

Dr Cooper left the question hanging too long, his eyes cast down towards his notes. Alec felt he'd touched a nerve.

"The Laird found her. I was called to assess her: unfortunately she was already dead."

Alec sensed he'd trodden, however unintentionally, on a confidentiality issue, so brought the subject to a close. "Anyway, Doctor, I'm fine. I won't need any more sleeping pills; but I'll think about what you've said."

"Good, we needn't schedule another appointment then, but feel free to make one if the need arises."

Alec stood at the bar of the Poacher's Rest. The moderate hum of numerous conversations blended with the volume from a satellite sports channel playing on the bar's big screen TV. It was just what he needed; anything was better than the abnormal silence of his own home.

He thought about Dr Cooper's comments and knew what he'd said made sense. *It's okay to miss them, but there's no point in worrying about things I can't control... I can't force Eileen to come home; she has to decide that for herself. And when she does I need to be able to offer more of a future, but how?* The question reverberated in his head but there wasn't an easy answer.

The door opened, Alec glanced at the two men who'd entered. Each dressed in suit and tie they stood out from the rest of the bar's clientele. The barman produced two pints of Best in response to no more than a raised eyebrow. The new arrivals paid and retired to a seat in the corner snug, just three feet behind Alec. That they kept their voices low only encouraged Alec to listen more intently.

"So what did you make of the discussion on the ring tonight?"

"It sticks in the throat, I know. But I think we made the only practical decision possible. We gifted it to him, so it's no longer Council property. If he buries it with her then that's his prerogative."

"But, Tony, it's valued in six figures. What will people think when they realise we stood by while 300 years of local heritage was buried forever?"

"Well, would you want to be the one to ask him to return a gift ... at a time like this? Besides we've more than had a return on it given the media interest last year. But moreover, the publicity we'll get in burying it with her will perpetuate the tourist interest. In the long term it's worth more to us buried than returned. After all, if we got it back we'd have to pay for its insurance and upkeep."

"I understand the insurance saving but where does the publicity come from?"

"In time, we'll promote walking tours of the town and they'll culminate at the grave. Can't you see? It closes a circle for us. It marries historic Ullemere with the recent past – something people will relate to. We'll be a fixture on the tourist map. We've commissioned a concrete plinth and once it's been laid over the grave, we'll go public."

Alec downed the remains of his beer and headed home. The seeds of an idea were sprouting, but he wasn't sure he liked it.

"Shit." Alec threw back the quilt and sat bolt upright in bed. A silvery half-light filtered through the bedroom window and played off the dust particles scattered by his sudden movement. His body glistened with beads of perspiration.

He'd rejected his idea from the Poacher's Rest. But, like a dog with an itch, his mind returned to rake it over. And each time his resolve weakened until it became that bit more plausible, that bit less ... abhorrent.

He headed for the shower; it'd freshen him up, maybe help him to sleep. The water was lukewarm. He closed his eyes and replayed the eavesdropped conversation as the water cascaded over him, cleansing him of his anxiety-induced sweat. He thought of Eileen, of the empty space in his bed and of his hurt at her disappointment in him as a provider. The water washed away the last lingering doubts and his eyes snapped open. This was a chance to build a better future for his family, maybe the only one he'd get, and he was going to take it.

The crowds began to form about an hour before the funeral. Spaces outside the Kirk filled first, until slowly the streets that quarter mile between Kirk and Cemetery became lined with people. A thousand voices filled the air with a steady buzz.

The Laird's silver Range Rover appeared in the distance and carefully picked its way toward the Kirk: a wave of hush sweeping before it. As it neared, flowers rained upon the ground, strewn from the open sunroof of the vehicle. But the car didn't stop at the Kirk. Onlookers stared at the darkened windows as it glided past and continued on towards the motorway. In its wake, the road lay littered with dozen upon dozen of red roses. The chatter built again until the funeral cortège came into view, wending down from the Laird's Estate.

Alec watched the burial from a vantage point afforded him by his duties. Only family and local dignitaries attended the graveside; members of the public watched from the cemetery gates. Several Town Councillors acted as pall-bearers. The Laird's relatives were elderly and few in number, but as an orphan, there were no family to mourn the Laird's wife, which Alec thought particularly sad. All the more reason, he thought, for the Laird to have put grief on-hold and been there for her; but then again, Alec knew it was possible to love someone so much as to be unable to face such finality as this.

When the last of the funeral party had departed the crowds all but evaporated and Alec was free to go about his duties. He knelt at the graveside, unfolded a piece of cloth and made a mental note of the screw-heads on the casket. Then he cast the cloth along its length, stood and began the infill.

By 3am Alec had returned to the graveside and laid groundsheets on the surrounding grass. He put aside his torch and screwdriver and set to work with his spade under the light of a quarter moon. His hands trembled: his stomach was a knot. The soil though was soft having been freshly dug and the eerie silence lent him speed and strength of purpose. Sweat soon poured from his brow to be wiped on his sleeve at increasingly shorter intervals, whilst his T-shirt became so wet it was almost a second skin. The inside of his mouth grew dry whilst his heart pumped so hard he felt sure it'd awaken the town.

His eyes surveyed the cemetery as each shovelful was expelled onto the groundsheets.

After 30 minutes' intense effort he reached the coffin and recovered the lint cloth. He cut a foothold in the grave wall either side of the casket before throwing out his spade and grabbing his torch and screwdriver. One by one he removed the screws from the lid and placed them in his pocket before reaching out to set down his tools.

With a foot in either foothold, he bent to grasp the lid. He slid it about an inch to the left and released it, then brought his left foot back across the lid to stand on the exposed casket lip. With his heart hammering inside his chest he took two deep breaths then lifted the lid away resting it between the grave's sidewall and the outer lip of the casket.

A shiver ran through him as he glimpsed the shroud-wrapped corpse for the first time. He grabbed the torch again and lowered himself until he knelt astride the coffin, balancing precariously on the casket lips. Once on, the torch beam exaggerated the dankness of the sidewalls and cast flickering shadows that drew the walls tight around him. His exhaled breath, still hot from his efforts, appeared as gaseous clouds swallowed whole by the grave's chilling darkness.

He cast the light across the torso of the corpse, seeking a fold in the shroud. Trembling, he leant forward and tugged exposing the left hand. He gawped. The hand was rough, the fingers stubby and pale. His mind raced ahead of him, his breaths short and sharp. The hairs on the back of his neck prickled. He raised the torchlight to the corpse's head and drew aside the shroud. It slipped silently from its host and the torch fell from his grasp. He made to stand but lost his balance falling backward to land with a thud at the foot of the coffin. He sat, wide-eyed, staring back at the pale, illuminated face of the Laird of Ullemere.

"I'd have spared you that, had I got here in time, Alec."

"Jesus," Alec said, his arms shooting back into the adjacent grave walls. He looked up to see Dr Cooper staring back at him. "Doctor?"

"I'm sorry I startled you, I can explain but first, let's afford the Laird some dignity and set the lid back on."

Alec was numb, but he stumbled across the frame of the coffin and retrieved his torch from under the chin of the Laird's lifeless face. He lowered the lid back into position and managed to refit the screws despite a now steady shake to his hands. When he was done, the doctor proffered his hand and pulled him out.

"Why have you done this?" the doctor asked, his eyes scanning the cemetery.

Alec hesitated, but there seemed little point in being anything but truthful now that he'd been caught. "I'd heard the Laird's wife was to be buried with the Ullemere Ring. I knew it was valuable and thought selling it would provide the new start Eileen and I needed."

"You weren't expecting to find the Laird's body then? Good God, man, I can't imagine the shock finding him must've been. Are you okay?"

"Never mind that," Alec said. "Why are you here and what happened to the Laird?"

"I'll explain while you put things back in order. But be quiet, we don't want to draw attention."

Alec took the spade and began to refill the grave keeping a wary eye on Dr Cooper.

.

The doctor took a deep breath. "I'd taken a chance with the burial and wanted to be sure suspicions hadn't been aroused. I had the cemetery watched and was alerted when you arrived."

"And the Laird?"

"I've been a frequent visitor to the Laird's estate since the wedding. Amelia, the Laird's wife, suffered a series of mishaps. I patched her up and she eventually confided in me. The Laird was prone to temper tantrums and would lash out at her. Amelia and I became close over the months and we discussed how best to free her from what was becoming a violent marriage. She believed he'd only let her go if he thought her dead."

Alec stopped shovelling. "Did you murder the Laird?"

"Of course not. Amelia needed my help. He'd struck her with his shooting stick. She was conscious but very distressed. She said she'd taken Tetraodontoxin, given to her by a friend from her native Haiti, and that she'd let loose a horse from the stables and would wait there for me. It was a race against time because what she'd taken was highly toxic, extremely dangerous."

"It's a poison, then?" Alec asked.

"It's the toxin of the puffer fish. Absorbed into the skin, it acts on the neurological system, causing paralysis, a decreased heart rate and a weak pulse. It's fatal more often than not, but if the victim survives 24 hours the chances are good. In the early stages though the victim appears dead and is in fact fairly close. The Laird found Amelia in this condition at the stables. I was nearby knowing he'd call."

"Okay, so you fooled the Laird but what of the undertakers and the authorities?"

"Easier than you think in a place this small, Alec. I'd signed the death certificate, liaised with the police and corroborated the riding accident theory with the Procurator Fiscal. I convinced the Fiscal that a postmortem would serve no purpose. The Laird agreed to have the body remain at the house when I suggested to him that it might avoid awkward questions. He thought he'd killed her – and in truth he might have if he'd continued. The Laird holds a lot of sway in a small community such as ours, Alec. He kept the undertaker at arms length and played the devastated husband. The undertaker was barely allowed to measure up."

Alec took a momentary rest from his labours. "But why would an undertaker not realise the body wasn't dead, even at a glance?"

The doctor nodded and again cast an eye around the cemetery. "Tricky, but undertakers see dead bodies all the time. Amelia's bruises would have seemed consistent with lividity – the pooling of blood upon death. Between the Laird's insistence upon their limited activity, and with my involvement, it passed as no more than a little eccentricity."

"So the undertaker didn't suspect?"

"No. Amelia was placed in an open casket, but we never thought to remove her ring. I suppose the undertaker noticed. I had the Laird seal the coffin, he didn't object. Seeing Amelia like that was a constant reminder of his callousness. But left alone I re-opened it and treated Amelia with oxygen and drugs to support her blood pressure. Once she'd recovered we filled the coffin with books bound in sheets. However, we were almost undone when, two days before the funeral, the Laird got himself exceedingly drunk and fell down the cellar stairs – breaking his neck."

Alec put the finishing touches to the refilled grave. "So, if the Laird's death was an accident, why was the switch necessary? In his case, wouldn't the truth have been simpler?"

"Perhaps, but two accidents inside a week? It posed too many questions and without the Laird's intervention the undertakers would want to attend properly to both bodies. We couldn't take the chance. So we removed the books and placed the Laird in the coffin: although he was a much tighter fit. I thought I was saving Amelia, Alec, it wasn't meant to become so complicated."

Alec collected the tools and rolled up the groundsheets. "But the Laird was seen before the funeral throwing roses along the cortège's path."

From behind came the sound of another voice. "That was me, but people will presume if it was the Laird's car it had to be him they saw drive off."

Alec spun around to see a hooded figure seated on a sarcophagus several feet away. The figure stood and walked to join them, removing the hood at the last moment.

Alec recognised Amelia; tall and slim, she moved with a graceful elegance that set her apart. Her dark and sultry complexion was undoubtedly attractive, but he winced at the sight of the wound to her forehead.

"I was saying my own goodbye to a husband I loved, despite his failings," Amelia said with an unmistakable lilt. She pulled the Ullemere Ring from her finger and held it out to Alec. "I wasn't sure about a man who'd have robbed my corpse for this. But it's not been mine for long and if relinquishing it can bring a local family back together then maybe it's a fitting end."

Alec hesitated. "Things have changed. I'm not sure I can be party to what you've both done."

"It's not a bribe, Alec," the doctor said. "You can report this if you wish. You'll have to explain how you found out, but we'd not think badly of you. If Amelia gives you the ring, either way, it's yours."

Alec thought for a second. He'd already had this battle with his conscience and in a few days time the plinth would seal the grave forever. But Amelia moved forward and placed it in his palm, wrapping his fingers around it.

"Thank-you…" Alec said, "…but what now?"

Dr Cooper took Amelia's hand. "Amelia leaves tonight, but I'll work my notice at the Health Centre before joining her. You know, Alec, our situations aren't that different. For us both love and temptation have been tightly bound, our conventional beliefs of right and wrong challenged. I don't think love would put us through this unless the goal was worthwhile."

Amelia fetched a single red rose she'd left on the sarcophagus and placed it on the Laird's grave. She reached into her purse and handed Alec a folded notepaper.

"I wrote this whilst you two talked earlier. Just in case." She pulled up her hood, then she and Dr Cooper left as quietly as they'd arrived.

"Good luck," Alec whispered.

Once again the cemetery was silent and Alec was alone. He unfolded the note. Under the Laird's letterhead was written a Bill of Sale for the Ullemere Ring, signed by Amelia and predating her 'death.'

HORRIBLE HEGARTY SPITS BLOOD

Susan Stern

My name is Rafael Brown but everyone calls me Rafi, thank God.

I dreaded going into Year Six with Mrs Hegarty. I didn't tell anyone of course, but I was right. After four days in her class, I hated her.

Today (day 236) was my worst ever. We were writing a story about a trip to Blackpool. I had just finished when I could feel Horrible Hegarty leaning over me. Like a giraffe with her long nose and huge glasses. She always starts talking very quietly, then she bellows down your ear.

'Rafael Brown,' she whispered, 'what do we always say?'

(I really hate being called Rafael. It makes me want to … crawl under the table.)

'Begin with a capital letter and end with a full stop,' I muttered, staring at my knees. Someone giggled. It was Lily Jones who sits opposite me. Silly cow.

'This is not a laughing matter, madam,' Mrs Hegarty roared.

She picked up my book and held it out so that everyone could see.

'There is one capital letter at the beginning of your work and one full stop at the end. There is an entire page of, doubtless, fascinating and inventive writing, without so much as a comma in between. So where is all that beautiful punctuation?'

I said the first thing that came into my head. 'I forgot, Mrs Hegarty.'

'You *forgot*?' She plonked the book down and it fell open on another page. This was covered with her red pen. Like drops of red spit, everywhere. She has spat blood on every page of my book.

She leaned over the table and glared at me with her yellowy eyes. Then she straightened up and said, 'You are in Year Six. By now, punctuation should be written on your heart.' She turned to the class, and said, 'However, to help Rafael remember, we shall all repeat it together. *You*, in particular, Rafael Brown.'

Everyone chanted, 'When you write a sentence, you begin with a capital letter and end with a full stop.'

'Good,' said Horrible Hegarty. 'Go back to your work, everyone. Rafael, come out to me.'

I walked slowly to her desk. She was wearing a red jumper and black trousers and smelt of the mints she sucked all the time. There was the roll of *Polos,* next to her navy blue pencil case. But underneath that minty smell there was something else, something sour, a bit like a mouldy old onion. I never found out what it was, but I certainly tried not to stand too close.

I handed her my storybook. She opened it and smoothed it out with her hands. Then she scratched in all the capitals and full stops and commas I had 'forgotten.' Suddenly, she stopped.

'What is this, Rafael?'

She stabbed two words with her pen.

'That's ice cream, Mrs Hegarty,' I muttered.

'And the other?'

'Beach.'

'They are so small and spiky, I can hardly read them. But they are indeed,' she peered at the page, then stared at me as though she'd never seen anything so awful, '*back to front.*'

Back to front? Oh no. I used to do that all the time when I was little – writing things back to front – because something weird just happened between my brain and my hand, but it had disappeared *completely* by the time I'd reached Year Five. Why had it started again? Of course I knew how to spell *ice cream* and *beach,* and *promenade*, half way down the page. She hadn't noticed it yet, but she would. I stepped back from the table, and keeping my eyes fixed on a crack in the floor, I waited.

I didn't wait long.

'Rafael, I have the solution.'

I looked up. Mrs Hegarty was leaning back in her chair and she was almost smiling. 'The psychologist said you should try using another medium, so take this pen.'

She held it towards me. I stared at it.

'On the board?'

'Yes. Off you go.'

I couldn't move. She waved the pen so close to my face, I had to take it. I still didn't move – I was praying for some instant magic that would make me disappear. Everyone had stopped talking and there was a deep silence in the classroom. Then someone laughed again.

'Quiet,' barked Mrs Hegarty.

In slow motion I turned to the board. I told myself to concentrate; told myself I *knew* how to spell those words. All I had to do was to say them over to myself, then I would write them.

I whispered under my breath: B e a c h. Okay. Now. Go for it.

I lifted my arm and began to write. The letters went down in a wiggly line, as though they were falling off the board…*c h e e b.*

Back to front. It had happened *again.* I glanced sideways at Horrible Hegarty but she didn't look at me, her yellowy-brown eyes still fixed on the board.

I took an enormous breath through my nose, recited the letters for i c e c r e a m to myself, then began to write. It came out like this: *m e e c r i c…*

Someone groaned.

There was no hope for me now. I had to finish; I had to escape. I felt the power of everyone's eyes like radar through my back. I scrawled *P r o n n a d e* under the other words, turned and handed the pen back to Horrible Hegarty.

My face was on fire.

'Well,' she said, 'that wasn't a great success, was it? Clearly I shall have to write them in your book, and you'll copy them out three times as usual. *Then* rewrite your story.'

I nodded.

'You'd better take a clean page and start all over again,' she added.

I crept back to my place. After a moment, people went on with their work and the buzz started again.

I copied out the words. I had just begun to rewrite my story, which by now I really hated, when the bell rang, and it was dinner-time.

I managed to forget about Horrible Hegarty during dinner. It was eggs, chips and beans, one of my best – then I played footie with the boys in my class. I've got better over the years, I'm on the school team now, midfield, on the right.

Then it was lessons and it all started again. Horrible Hegarty was droning on about an OFSTED inspection that was going to happen in a month's time, after the Easter holidays.

'Everyone, even our caretaker, Mr Ainsworth, will be observed. So remember, all your work will have to be absolutely excellent.'

Meanwhile, I was thinking about the diary that Gramps had given me at the weekend. 'It's last year's,' he'd said. 'Empty. Do what you like with it.'

I knew exactly what I'd use it for. Drawing cartoons. I really like doing them and I've done loads. I was thinking how I'd do one about a mad bloke who'd had a battle with a windmill. Gramps had told me about him, and I thought it would be a really great scene to…

'What did I just say, Rafael Brown?'

Oh no. I had no idea what she'd said. I looked at the people on my table. The girls just folded their lips. *Girls*. My mate, Anton, who sits next to Lily Jones, with his back to Hegarty, leaned over and whispered out of the corner of his lips, 'OFSTED.'

'OFSTED, Mrs Hegarty,' I said quickly.

'Right. And thank you, Anton, for helping Rafael answer.'

How does she know? She's a witch as well. I have no problem with burning witches if they're anything like her. After today, I would do it myself. Well, I suppose I wouldn't … but I really need some way of getting her off my back, because I'm really beginning to hate coming to school. I've had six months of Horrible, Hateful, *Hideous* Hegarty, and it's no joke. I have to find something.

The first chapter from Susan's novel Rafi Brown and the Kandi Floss Kid.

Your Genealogy

I watched your face barely change
as that feeling set in you
        like a lead doll invading your body
that you cannot change a single thing about the past
its essence smothered you from the inside out
and broke you in the shape of just one tear
that smeared down your cheek

and I wanted to wrap the whole of history
in a red blanket
and hide it from you
and cry so loud you'd never look again.

Anne Louise Kershaw

Battle of Instincts

I've strengthened my stomach muscles
by practicing the scales
   doe-rayed them into
a band like force
and elasticity in *me*
   from that solid and sinewy floor
I can propel a missile of sound
large enough
to hit as *far* as the back
wall of a school hall.

But I yearn
to stretch them beyond capacity
   like the jeans I grew out of
   once held a teen body
   became shaped
like an almost woman's arse!

Because there's something
that already exists
   not for breakfast or bleeding
   but for homing some genes
   for a brief time at least
while they bake to perfection
into their bronze yeasty skin
   and I'm desperately wanting to meet them

their already half real creation
with its bi-needy threat
of a loving invasion
   with man's ally would feed off my land
   its sponge-like absorbance
of time
would make my mine
not my *own* –
a half-time to share
between natives

I already now share with another
whose smooth seedy ally
is keen
            to create a coalition –
            our needy and loving invader!
Who I'm desperately wanting to meet now
to inhale their white pepper breath.

Anne Louise Kershaw

THE PENGUINS

Michelle Fryer

The door slammed shut and he appeared in the kitchen doorway. She had been waiting, simmering, all day. 'What happened?' he asked lazily.

'The bastard grill burnt my toast and that thing's been having a field day for the past ten minutes,' she snapped.

He reached up and silenced the blaring smoke alarm with his fist, then smiled with satisfaction at the cracked lid which lay on the floor at his feet. 'Well at least we know we'll never die in a fire, the way that thing goes on,' he said, turning to wander into the living room.

'You're dead already,' she muttered bitterly to his back. Then she followed him into the living room where he sat forlornly on the settee. He made no attempt to look up as she stood herself in front of him, instead studying the dirty trainers that lay to one side of his feet. She felt her face reddening with the anger which had been boiling inside her for weeks and she could not hold back any longer.

'What's up?' he asked timidly. She was making him nervous.

'Did you eat three Penguins last night?' She tried to conceal her rage behind her low tone but her gritted teeth gave her away.

'No,' he said simply, refusing to make eye contact.

'Yeah you did … you greedy bastard, 'cause there were 12 and now there's nine … and I've not had one.' She put her thumb to her mouth and bit it hard.

He shifted uncomfortably. 'Um … I thought I only had two,' he said, his eyebrow furrowed in thought.

'*It … was … three*,' she said slowly and precisely, tears of anger welling in her eyes. She blinked hard. Her top lip curled into a snarl and her eyes burnt into his face, waiting.

'Maybe I did … I dunno. I wasn't counting or I lost count … I don't know …this is … going nowhere, I mean…' He began to trail off then added, helplessly, 'I'm sorry,' with a bewildered shrug.

Any response would have been unfavourable. She began her attack. 'There's nothing in the fridge but two cans of special brew,' she said slowly. 'We've had nothing but toast three times a day for the past fuck-knows how long. The rent's *late*. So the bank's gonna charge me for having no money because that makes sense… *You* can't get a job … the place is freezing… For Christ's sake, we're in such a mess and there you are … *you*, you're just … eating all the *fucking* Penguins.'

Her pointing finger wavered millimetres from his chest.

He laughed. 'Why you getting all flustered over Penguins? God…What's *happened* to you? You used to be so laid back, but now … now you're… I dunno … flipping over anything. I know times are bad but I really… I can't… There's no need for this.' He tore his eyes bitterly away from hers and gazed ahead.

.

Gesturing an arm to the unkempt space around them, she spoke with desperation. 'But look around though. Just look. Look at the state of this place.' Her eyes lowered to the rows of empty beer cans which stood proudly on the table. 'Is it any wonder I'm angry? Our lives are a mess and I feel like I'm getting nothing from you. Nothing at all. You're so … distant,' she said, helplessly. 'I mean what've you been doing all day? Where've you *been*?'

'Just around … I guess,' he mumbled.

His unresponsiveness was so frustrating. 'Have you even bothered looking for a job today?' she continued savagely.

'Job? Yeah I went to the job centre,' he said with satisfaction. Then his tone changed to annoyance. 'I go there every day. Up and down that long road… Every day, the same. That's what I do, isn't it? Go to the job centre and back… My life's ruled by the fucking job centre.'

His voice was slowly rising above hers, but she wasn't giving in yet.

'Yeah, and that's half the problem. That's *all* you do. Here I am, student-cum-housewife … rubbish at both... And there's you … what, half an hour in the job centre and you think you've done well? Barely off your arse then you're back here drinking your special brews or in the café gambling money you don't have on that internet poker.' Her words spewed out in a rant and she sighed with relief.

He stared at her, his mouth opening, attempting to form words he did not have. Frowning, he lowered his eyes to the floor.

'So what then?' she continued. Then seeing him swipe the ball of his hand over his moist eye, she looked away guiltily, her tone softening. 'You probably spoke to that Brian who probably convinced you *again* that none of the jobs were good enough for you? It's all right for him… He's got a bloody job, telling people how to get jobs. At least that's what he's supposed to do, not put them off the idea.'

He stroked his fingertips over his forehead. 'I didn't make it to Brian,' he mused, 'I was standing in the queue and there was a guy beside me… He was shifting about as though he couldn't decide whether he was in the queue or not, so I said, "You can go next mate." So then he says "Nah, I *work* here, mate." It was the way he said it… So bloody smug he was. As if he was better than me 'cause he had a job…'Cause he was doing his bit and that.' He started from his seat. '"*I work*!" Who did he think he was? And what's his fuckin' job anyway? Some sort of bouncer for job centre brawls? All suited and booted with his fucking walkie-talkie! He made me feel like shit, Alex.' He sat down heavily with a sigh, 'And I come back here and I'm getting aggro from you about eating too many chocolate bars. What's it all about?' He pulled his head back against the settee and gazed at the ceiling.

She momentarily clasped her hands to her face, then dropped herself onto the settee beside him. It had felt like an eternity since he had said her name. 'Don't you get it? It's not about the Penguins. They're just the tip of the iceberg,' she smiled, turning his face to look at hers with the tips of her fingers.

His eyes met hers for a second then dropped, his mouth expressionless.

She watched him fiddle with his fingers uncomfortably. 'It's about you and me,' she continued. 'We're worlds apart and I'm cracking up … going over the edge… I feel as though our lives are in ruins and you're so far away from me that I can't reach you…When're you going to come back to me?'

He stared past her, out of the window. He didn't know the way back and he resented *her* for it. 'It's all about *you*,' he said, pulling her hand from his face. Then he rose from the settee, and shifted silently past her.

'Where you going?' she asked, but he didn't respond. Sitting back against the settee, she hugged her knees to her chest.

Later she could hear the wardrobe doors closing in the bedroom. She wanted to go in there but instead rested her chin on her knees and gazed out of the window. Several minutes passed, her like this and him gathering things from the bedroom. Then he appeared in the doorway. She slowly turned round, her eyes dropping to the holdall that hung from his hand. For a few seconds both were transfixed by the bag. He was the first to speak. 'I'm going to stay at Chris' for a bit,' he mumbled, twisting the bag handle awkwardly.

She looked pleadingly at his face, silently asking if he would be back.

His shrug gave her the answer she both expected and dreaded.

'Jack … please … can't we just…?' The words trailed off, her voice a whisper choked with tears. She gave in to her pain and buried her face in her crossed arms.

'I just can't … I'm sorry but … I *can't*…' he said, turning to the door.

She looked up in time to see him quietly close it behind him.

He stood for a few seconds in the hallway, half wishing he could go back in but knowing he couldn't. He knew they had both changed too much and what they had before could not be clawed back.

She looked at the shut door, willing the 'old' Jack to come back in. She couldn't fathom how they had drifted so far away from one another.

The flat door closed and in seconds he was downstairs, out of the front door, and she was watching him as he walked past the window.

He didn't look up, but made his way down the road, his eyes watching his feet. She stared at his back as he trod distance between them.

GOODBYE LONGFELLOW ROAD

Rachel Broady

Pat was packing his bags, really fast like adults did on the telly after a row.

He was biting his bottom lip. I saw tears fall onto the khaki sack he was filling with books and pamphlets. He shoved his work boots inside as I stood at the door of his room, watching.

The sun glared through the thin curtain making the walls and posters turn blue. One poster had a drawing of a man wearing a gas mask, his eyes covered with Union Jacks. Next to that was the Irish Declaration of Independence. It was in a dusty frame, all scratched and faded. The others I'd seen had always been new and not creased. I read the last bit.

'We ask His Divine blessing on this the last stage of the struggle we have pledged ourselves to carry through to freedom.'

Directly above his bed there was a poster that said 'Loose Talk Costs Lives' and underneath it read 'what ever you say, say nothing.' I imagined the whispered conversations he'd had with mum.

Pat walked over to his dressing table to get his bottle of Brut. Mum had bought it him for Christmas. He reached for it then leaned against the wall and his shoulders shook. I heard the gentle sobs he was trying to hide.

"I'm sorry you're going," I said.

He spun round, wiping his face with his palms and forcing a smile.

"Oh, I'll be fine." He walked back to the bed and started packing his stuff again. "Don't you be worrying about me."

He winked but, as he did, a tear fell down his face. He laughed and wiped it away.

"I'll really miss you," I said. "I wish you didn't have to go." I kicked my foot against the door frame.

I walked in and picked up the bottle of aftershave for him. There was a picture of St Christopher next to it, wrapped tight in plastic to protect it from damage. I passed that to him too.

He kissed my forehead.

"You've been like—" I stopped. I took a breath. "You've been like my dad. Only better."

"Your dad loves you, you know that," he said. "And so do I."

He slumped onto the bed. He put his head in his hands.

I sat next to him. I could feel the sun on my back.

"I'm gonna miss you, kid," he said, when he came up for air. "You look after yourself, you hear? Study hard. Look after others. And don't be taking any shite from anyone."

It reminded me of the talks he gave to me when we first met, his hands on my shoulders, like he was trying to drill the information into my brain with his blue eyes.

I took his hand. It was wet. "I know what you do, you know."

"I should think you do by now," he said, looking around his room. I smiled up at the cross above his bedroom door. "Old habits," he said.

The cabinet his mum had brought for him was standing in the corner, a thick layer of dust on the top, books on the bottom shelf, papers on the middle one.

"How're you going to get that away?" I asked.

"I'm not," he said. "Do you want it?"

"Not really," I said. "It's ugly."

"It is that," Pat said. "And it's of no use to me."

"Will you come back for it?"

"I doubt that very much."

"So, when you're gone, you're gone for good."

"It's better that way."

He stood up and swung the huge bag over his shoulder and grabbed his leather jacket off the bed.

"I'd better be going. Will you say goodbye to your ma for me?"

I stayed close to him as we walked downstairs, nearly tripping him up. I wished I was still small enough to curl up in his lap or big enough to go with him. He turned around at the bottom of the stairs. He kissed the top of my head.

"You look after yourself, now." His voice was muffled by my hair.

"I will if you will." I tried to laugh but it sounded like a squeak. Then we both laughed properly.

Sitting on the doorstep, I watched him leave. He walked fast, shoulders straight, the sun shining on his jacket. He didn't look back. When he turned the corner I stared after him, then closed my eyes, wanting to remember the moment he left. I remembered dad there too. I looked at the houses opposite and tried to remember everyone who had been and gone on the street. Only Rat Woman stayed in her house with her fig rolls.

I decided to sit outside until my eyes weren't red anymore but I needed the toilet so I ran straight through the house and into the back yard. I sat holding my feet above the floor and would've been embarrassed about my big trump but my belly was aching and only the stray cats in the yard could hear me. The toilet wouldn't flush when I'd finished. I closed the door so that the cats didn't have to smell it.

"So that's him gone then," mum said when I went into the living room. I could tell she'd been crying.

It was really dark. The dirty windows stopped the sun getting in. Mum was on the settee with a blanket wrapped around her shoulders, playing with the foil from inside a cigarette packet. She used to make little wine glasses with the foil and stand them on the fireplace.

"He says he won't visit," I said.

"Well, he's honest, I'll give him that."

"Why's he gone?" I asked.

"I'm thinking we should go back to Manchester, back to your dad. What do you think?"

Mum wiped her eyes, picked her glasses up from the arm of the chair to put them on.

"I don't know," I said.

"You've missed your dad."

I didn't say anything.

She picked up her tea and drew her hands tight around the mug, her fingers laced through the handle and her knuckles white. I could see the top of the women's sign above her hand.

"He's not coming back ever, is he?" I asked, sitting next to her. I put my hand across my belly to try to stop the aching.

"I wouldn't bet on it," mum said. She lifted her mug to her lips. Her glasses steamed. She swallowed her tea and took a deep breath. "People will always let you down," she said. She looked at me and forced a smile. "You have to remember, love, no single individual can love you as much as you want. You have to rely on your class…"

I watched her mouth as she spoke. It moved quickly, the inside of her lips creasing and straightening. Her lips stuck to her front teeth until she licked the dryness away. She moved her hands as she spoke, splashing tea from the mug that she moved from one hand to the other and back again. Her hands were shaking.

"Pat's in our class," I said.

"He is, yes… Oh, not now, love," she said, putting her mug on the floor and her head in her hands. "Go on out and play."

"I've got belly ache."

"Well, go and lie on the floor on your belly, that'll shift it."

I sat on the doorstep and watched the ants. The street was almost empty now.

As mum came in the front door, she struggled to get her breath, clutching her hand to her chest as she moved.

"What's wrong mum? Where've you been?" I asked. Rat Woman came running in behind her. Her hair looked even messier than usual.

"What is it?" she said to mum. "What on Earth has got you into this mess? I've been watching you like this all the way up the street."

Mum groaned loudly and held on to the wall, like she was blind and couldn't find the living room door.

"Who's that fella following you?" Rat Woman said looking quickly towards the front door. "What's going on?"

We followed mum into the living room.

"What's wrong, mum?" I said, reaching for the hem of her cheesecloth top. "Please, mum. What's wrong?"

She looked back at me. She closed her eyes briefly like they ached and she couldn't hold them open. She touched my face and wandered into the living room, falling into her chair. She gripped the arms, and she looked up at me through bloodshot eyes.

"It's Pat," she said. "Pat."

She stopped speaking, like her crooked mouth couldn't get the words out properly. Her whole face crumpled and she cried again.

Rat Woman's hands were knotted in front of her body until, when mum's loud gasp broke the silence, she leapt forward and fell to her knees, wrapping her arms around mum and squeezing her. She squeezed her eyes closed at the same time and fat tears fell down her cheeks too.

"What's wrong with Pat?" I said, sliding down the doorframe. I waited for mum to stop crying and tell me he was dead.

"He went back to Ireland," mum told Rat Woman when she'd calmed down a bit. "Only for a few days but he was shot by soldiers when his mum's home was raided. They'd been after him for years, of course, and he wouldn't have gone back if—"

"The poor wee fella," Rat Woman said in a pretend Irish accent. Mum didn't get mad, she just looked at me and burst into tears. I didn't move from my space by the door. I clutched my knees to my chest and felt the pain in my throat as I struggled not to cry. Pat would've told me to be strong. He would've told me to be strong for mum. I watched Rat Woman hold her hand.

I noticed that the man Rat Woman had seen was still outside. He shuffled about for ages before walking into the hall. I couldn't make out his face, the light from outside put him in a shadow. He took a step closer. He had skinny arms. His hands were tight in the pockets of his jeans and the sun shone through the gap in his legs as he walked towards me. He tugged a hand from his pocket and pushed his long hair away from his face as he reached me.

"I'm James," he said. "Pat's brother."

He kneeled down next to me and I could see Pat's blue eyes. James' were grey around the outside but he had crow's feet that were so big they almost reached his ears. Laugh lines, mum called them.

"Me ma sent us," he said. "Well, we both thought someone should be with you. It was easier for me to get here, she's getting on you know and…" He stroked my face and the lines by his eyes stretched wide.

"I'd better make everyone a cup of tea," Rat Woman said, standing up and wiping her front like she was wearing a pinny.

James looked her up and down, then looked at me almost laughing. "That'd be lovely," he said, watching her as she wandered down the hall.

"She's a bit mad," I said.

"Aye, she may be," he said. "But she looked after your ma well enough just now." He ruffled my hair as he got up to go to mum.

"What about the funeral?" mum said. "What was it like?"

James went to answer and stopped.

"How's your poor mum," she said. "What was going on? How did they get him?"

James listened and didn't say a word.

Mum looked up at him. "Why did this happen?"

"It's like I said. They were after him for years. He wouldn't have had it any other way."

Mum shook her head at that, like he was talking daft. "I did love him," she said, almost as if James had said she didn't. "He never gave me a single reason not to."

"I know," he said. "And he knew."

Mum looked as if she had another question but curled up instead, her knees to her chest. James sat by her and she buried her sobs in his shoulder.

I crept upstairs to get the piece of paper from under my mattress and then out into the street. James was holding mum's hand as I passed the door, rocking backwards and forwards, making her chair creak.

I ran towards the end of the street. I ran for so long I had to open my mouth to breath. I wasn't allowed to cross the main road to get to the phone box but mum hadn't seen me leave. I dialled the number Carol had given me and had to do it twice when my finger slipped out of the hole and dialled the wrong number. The phone box smelled of wee and there were phone numbers written all over the glass. An old woman waited outside while I dialled, tutting when I made a mistake and had to do it again. She stood nearer the door as I listened to Carol's phone ringing. She sounded groggy when she answered.

"It's mum," I said "Pat."

"What is it? Where are you?"

"I need you to come home."

"I'm sorry, love, but mum doesn't want me there, does she?"

"She will. Please. Pat's dead."

Extracts from a novel.

Old Hag

Caged in her fortress of pillows
I succumb to, and don't fear, the light.

Smothered under her thunders
and bloody skies, I hear the light

vibrating. Pushing and pulling
my silvery thread near the light –

the puppet of the night, whose tears
could never clear the light.

She taught me silence, not to scream,
to struggle, not to smear the light

and feel 5,000 souls crush me
with their foggy and nuclear light.

But patient and pinned and cold
I wait, to break the new frontier of light.

Carley Moulton

Fear

He creeps in, the stench of sewers
that seems to rise from nowhere.
A reminder of the strength I lack
to create a gap between us; of how
human I am, and caged by him
the darker twin. I stare.

Flesh blood and skin we share all
but the food (*he eats at dark
to set my heart racing*). We glare
into similar eyes, in the mirror.
His hooded figure hanging on
fine familiar fog disappears
with the thumping blood
as I turn the lights on.

Carley Moulton

RORY

Cathryn Freear

Rory was a green and blue dinosaur who sat at the end of Toby's bed and protected him from various baddies. These included monsters, ghosts, invading pirates with one eye and hooks for hands, sharks, and most recently a terrible half-woman half-spider creature called Morag. She had begun to stalk Toby shortly after he watched a film about her on television, probably because she knew that he was on to her now.

Rory did not always sit at the end of the bed. Sometimes, when the baddies had gone quiet for a while, Toby let Rory get under the covers with him and would toss a small, chubby arm around his furry bodyguard, clinging tightly to him until sleep loosened his grip. Rory liked these times. He enjoyed snuggling close to Toby, feeling loved and listening to the sounds of the little boy breathing. He could not relax completely of course since he was still on guard and baddies could be sneaky.

At other times, when the baddies were being particularly fearsome, Rory had to leave the bed entirely and bravely enter their secret hideouts to scare them into staying away from Toby. Mostly these hideouts were in the usual places such as under the bed or in the wardrobe but, as I mentioned, baddies can be sneaky. Morag, for example, scaled the walls of the house to climb up to Toby's window and witches often flew right up to it on their broomsticks. This meant that Rory had to spend some nights on the windowsill ready to push Morag back down and bite the wicked witch's hands.

Several times Toby had heard the tapping of claws and slithering of scaly flesh making its way down the hallway towards his bedroom. On these occasions Rory had been forced to stand guard outside Toby's bedroom door all night and he didn't mind admitting that he had felt quite scared himself. The hallway was long, narrow and dark and Rory wasn't able to see very far along it. Dinosaurs have exceptionally good hearing however, and Rory's heart had fluttered, sunk and skipped beats at the foreboding sounds of the varnished floorboards creaking under the weight of huge hairy beasts, or at the rustle of the curtains as vengeful ghosts swept behind them. Nevertheless, Rory had stood his ground, glaring ferociously into the blackness through his glassy orange and black eyes, baring his pointy, white felt teeth and every now and then emitting a low growl as a warning to the waiting baddies who had obviously been afraid since they kept their distance.

Baddies do not come out during the day because they are all asleep. Besides, they know that if they did you could easily spot them sneaking up on you and get an adult. This meant that Rory was free to play games with Toby in the daytime and sometimes to go on adventures.

Rory always went with Toby on adventures, partly because he was so strong and ferocious, but also because Toby loved him best of all his toys. That is not to say, however, that Toby in any way neglected his other toys. Rory was frequently joined by other toy box acquaintances. He got along well with most of them and enjoyed having someone else to chat to, but he did find that Martin the hedgehog got quite tiresome after a while, due to his constant low spirits.

These had been brought on the previous summer when Martin had fallen from Toby's grasp onto a picture that he had been painting earlier in the day. The paint was still wet since it had been a particularly colourful painting of Toby, his parents and Rory at the seaside. Martin was unfortunate enough to fall on the portion depicting the smiley yellow sun. His bad luck continued in the fact that Toby's mum was out that day with a friend and Toby's dad, having been presented with a sticky yellow hedgehog and the word 'dirty' looked down into his son's expectant face and decided that, to prevent any drama, he had better figure out how to use the washing machine.

After much grunting and swearing from Toby's dad, Martin had found himself spinning round and round with some towels in lukewarm soapy water. When he emerged half an hour later, the yellow paint had completely vanished, but unfortunately his once beautiful fur spikes had become clumped together and no amount of coaxing with a comb on the part of Toby's mum could return them to their former glory.

Martin's ego took a real battering that day and, despite his fellow toys' best efforts to restore his spirits, he had never been the same since. Rory had, at first, felt sorry for Martin and tried along with the other toys to make him happy again, but Martin would not be budged from his depressive state and his constant gloominess began to infect some of the other toys. His many reminiscences about the days when he had had beautiful spikes started to annoy Rory and he felt happier when Martin didn't join he and Toby. Even Martin's depression, however, was preferable to Rory than the insufferable arrogance of the plastic warrior machine Victor Prime.

Victor had arrived the previous Christmas and instantly made himself unpopular with all the other toys because of his egomania, but most especially with Rory who found, to his horror, that Victor was now to assist him in protecting Toby at night. Rory tolerated Victor's constant showing off for several weeks. He feigned interest when Victor showed him the plastic guns attached to his arms and told him how many rounds they were capable of firing per minute and pretended to be impressed when Victor related in great detail the many battles he claimed to have fought and won against creatures known as Morfs, of whom Rory had never heard. Eventually however, Rory's patience began to wear thin. He became ruder and ruder to Victor until eventually he just stopped speaking to him altogether. Victor at first seemed unperturbed, obviously interpreting Rory's silence for intense interest and concentration. He realised that this was not the case when Rory's continued silence one night caused Victor to question, "Hey Rory, are you listening? I was telling you about the time I took on six Morfs single handed." To which Rory's reply was so vehemently angry it should not be repeated. Suffice to say that he made his feelings about listening to any more of Victor's stories very clear and threatened him with great pain should he try to relate any more.

From that night on Victor was a very quiet companion and Rory was extremely thankful for it until he began to notice Victor's increasing fear. Victor, who had previously remained unshaken by the antics of the baddies, now began to tremble at every creak and shuttle. The first time it happened Rory had felt secretly pleased and superior for remaining unafraid in the face of danger.

By assigning Victor as his partner, Toby had hurt Rory and although he still did his best to protect the little boy he couldn't help feeling some resentment towards him. It was not often that they fell out. True, Rory hadn't been pleased when Toby had coloured in his glass eyes with a black felt tip several years ago, but nothing had put nearly so much strain on their friendship as this Victor incident.

After a while Victor's increasing fear of the baddies began to worry Rory. He knew that if they sensed Victor's weakness they would not be so afraid to attack, then the pair of them, and worst of all Toby, would be in grave danger. Feeling quite guilty after his outburst at Victor, Rory was reluctant to broach the subject of the warrior machine's nerves, but when one night Victor trembled so hard on the end of Toby's bed that he was in danger of toppling off it, Rory decided that he would have to say something.

"You all right there Victor?"

Victor's first reaction to the sound of Rory's voice was to jump in fear, but once he saw the look of concern on the dinosaur's face he collapsed onto the bed with his knees bent and head in his hands then, in a sobbing voice, released all his pent up fears in a great stream of speech.

"Oh no, no I'm not all right. I'm scared, really scared all the time. I never was before but, but after you shouted at me that time," here Victor peered nervously at Rory through his plastic fingers obviously fearful of angering the dinosaur again, but Rory merely looked guilty and worried so Victor continued, "well you were so scary and I thought that if you frightened me that much then how on earth was I going to fight off all these baddies? I mean, you're a dinosaur and you've been scaring them for years, but I'm just a robot man, not a real warrior. I've never really fought anyone. I lied about the Morfs," he said looking guiltily at Rory's confused expression. "My guns don't really work either," he sobbed.

Feeling very small and guilty Rory attempted to comfort his companion. "It doesn't matter about your guns – you just have to look scary. The baddies are cowards really. Don't feel bad for getting scared. I do too sometimes."

Victor peered up from his sobs. "Really? You get scared?"

"Well, yes, sometimes," Rory confessed feeling awkward. Victor looked slightly happier for a moment before shaking his head and returning to his dejected state.

"Not as scared as me you don't. I keep thinking about that orange and brown monster Toby told us to watch out for – the one that lives under the bed and bites off your toes if they stick out of the covers. He's enormous, Toby said. I could never stand up to him."

"Of course you could."

"No, no I couldn't. I don't want to do this any more." Victor was finally consumed by his misery and sank his head into his knees, rocking back and forth.

"All right, all right, don't worry. I'll speak to Toby about it tomorrow. He'll understand. I promise."

Victor looked significantly happier at this and although he remained sitting hugging his knees, he had stopped crying and rocking.

"Victor."

"Yes?"

"I'm sorry."

"S'alright Rory. I suppose I just wasn't meant to be a warrior or a protector. I actually like animals more."

Rory felt quite anxious about speaking to Toby concerning Victor's removal as a protector, not because he thought that Toby would mind Victor being scared; in fact he would completely understand, being quite a nervous boy himself. What worried Rory was Toby's reaction when he discovered that it was Rory's fault that Victor was scared. Would he be very angry? Would he remove Rory as his protector too for being so mean? That would be awful!

Fortunately for Rory, Victor saved him the trouble entirely by jumping so hard later that night when a window slammed in the bathroom that he finally did fall off of the bed. When Toby found him on the floor the next morning he realised Victor's inadequacy for the protector job and, after giving him a hug and a friendly pat, placed him, to Victor's great delight, on the shelf amongst the plastic farm animals on their felt farm where he stayed happily for some time.

'Jus' you now," Toby said, picking up his favourite dinosaur and smiling.

Rory beamed proudly and happily back at him showing the pointy felt teeth that had terrified so many baddies. That was just the way he liked it.

TESTIFY

Charlotte Anne Clegg

"Please! Don't! I won't tell. Please!" cried Christopher.

The child pleaded with his captor, a figure dressed all in black. Beautiful blonde hair was plastered to his head, streaked with sweat and blood. Tears no longer fell from clear blue eyes; eyes which reflected extreme terror and pain. Bone protruded through the pale skin of his left leg. Whimpering, he tried again.

"Please! Stop it! No more, please!"

The figure stood above him, laughing, and in answer to his pleas stabbed him again in the leg. Christopher screamed and clutched at his wounds. Blood seeped through his fingers.

"That'll teach you *child*. Just keep nice and quiet and be a good boy, or I'll stick this knife straight through your little neck!"

Christopher tried not to make a sound. He held his breath, and squeezed his eyes tightly shut to try and subdue the pain. After a couple of minutes, he heard heavy footsteps walk out of the room and go downstairs. He listened intently, and when he could hear no more, he grappled along the floor until he came in contact with an arm. Christopher pulled it close to him, and held the clammy hands in his own.

"Carolyn," he whispered to his twin sister. "Carolyn, wake up. Come on, we need to hide."

Carolyn's blonde curls were almost unrecognisable, matted and dyed a dark shade of red. Her patent white shoes were scuffed, and the right foot was turned out at an odd angle.

"Carolyn, quick. We need to hide. We need to get away. Come on Carolyn. If you wake up, I'll give you my favourite teddy, come on now!" he said with more urgency.

Still Carolyn didn't move or make a sound. Her lips had started to take on a bluish tinge. Biting part of his jumper to stop himself crying out loud in agony, Christopher dragged Carolyn to the door of the bedroom, and out into the hall. With his free hand he used the banister to support himself, and yanked his sister to the bathroom. Once they were both inside, he locked the door.

Downstairs the figure in black prowled the living room, pausing over the mantelpiece. A photograph of the twins took pride of place in the centre. In the photo, Christopher and Carolyn looked like porcelain dolls with Cherub faced, delicate features, big crystal blue eyes and hair that glowed like strands of gold. With tiny button noses and peaches and cream skin, the seven year olds shone. On each side of the photo stood portraits of their parents, both equally beautiful; it was obvious to see were the children had got their looks from. The only characteristic that differed was that of their mother's striking turquoise eyes. The captor lifted up the photo of the twins, took it out of its frame, pocketed it, and let the frame drop to the floor. As it hit the floor it shattered, and shards of glass scattered across the room.

In the corner of the room a man was tied fast to a chair. A deep cut ran along the side of his head and blood oozed down his face. A pool of blood lay underneath the chair. He swayed from side to side and struggled to stay conscious.

"David," said the figure in black, pacing in front of him. "David"

"The children, the twins," David forced out. "Christopher. Carolyn. Please, where are they? What have you done?"

"Christopher. Carolyn," said the captor in mock concern. "Two darling little angels. It would be a shame if anything had happened to them." The captor sat opposite David and stared at him.

Swaying, David's eyes drifted towards the stairs, hoping to see some sign that his children were all right.

"David!" snapped the figure. "Time. Time! Never enough time, David. But now I'm in charge. I'm in charge of time. So you have no choice but to spend time on me!"

David was slapped across the face. The captor walked back over to the fireplace, pulled the clock off the wall and smashed it on the floor. Going back over to David and taking his watch, the tormentor smashed that too.

"Now, answer my question. Tell me why."

Unable to focus enough to answer the question, David's thoughts drifted back to his children, and his eyes once more wandered towards the stairs.

"Tell me why, David."

"Please. Christopher, Carolyn. Please, let me see that they're okay," begged David. "Please, I need to see them,"

Another slap connected with his cheek. A slap hard enough to knock over the chair he was tied to.

Picking him up again the figure said, "Let's have it your way, shall we. I'll fetch your angels."

In the bathroom, Christopher was still holding onto his sister. He was rocking from side to side, murmuring to himself and Carolyn.

"The bad one's gone away now. It's okay. Daddy's going to come and fix everything. Talk to me Carolyn, you don't need to pretend anymore. Daddy will make you better. The badness has gone now, wake up. Wake up and you'll see."

The captor started walking upstairs, exaggerating each step.

Christopher's heart jumped into his mouth. Holding Carolyn tighter he pushed himself into the corner.

Outside the bathroom, the footsteps made their way into the bedroom where the children had been tortured. Along the floor leading to the bathroom, a dark red streak marked the path that Christopher had pulled Carolyn along.

"Christopher. Daddy wants to see you both. Open the door, then Daddy can make Carolyn better."

Christopher's ears perked up.

"Daddy? Daddy, are you there?"

"Yes sweetheart, Daddy's waiting for you. Open the door."

Slowly Christopher pulled himself to the door, letting go of Carolyn for the first time since entering the bathroom. He unlocked the door, and opened it just enough to look out, up into the cold, calculating eyes of his captor. The dark figure stared down at the child, holding a knife glistening with blood.

Shaking with fear, Christopher repeated, "Daddy?"

The captor grabbed Carolyn's hair, snatched Christopher by the arm and dragged the children downstairs to present them to their father. Carolyn's doll-like body hung limply, and her knees made a cracking sound upon each stair. One of her shoes came off, revealing socks with tiny pink flowers embroidered around the top.

Christopher flinched with agony as his leg hit every step.

Upon reaching the bottom of the stairs, the figure shouted, "Oh, David! Your children are here to see you."

Christopher grasped his father's leg and cried out, "Daddy! You can fix Carolyn, can't you?"

David looked down at Christopher, and then across at Carolyn, and felt as though his heart had been ripped out. "What have you done to her?"

Shrugging, the figure said, "Perhaps now you'll listen to me and start talking, while you still have one child left." Walking to the other end of the room, the captor bent over a duffle bag, reached in and pulled out a hand gun. Moving back to where David and the twins where, the figure aimed the gun at the middle of David's head, and said, "Now, David. Tell *me WHY!*"

David, distraught with the thought that Carolyn lay dead at his feet, was unable to speak. Tears streamed down his face. Trying to hold them back, his mind screamed at him to talk, to promise anything just to make sure that Christopher wasn't murdered like his sister. Feeling Christopher holding tight to his leg and seeing him holding Carolyn's hand, he thought of him growing up without the sibling to whom he was so close, and broke down again.

The captor lowered the gun, and shot David in the knee cap.

Christopher screamed and struggled to his feet, using his writhing father as a source of support. Looking up at the figure he shouted, "Stop hurting us Mummy!"

An extract from the first chapter of a novel.

FLIGHT

Caroline Moir

After work she went into town to the large newsagents and bought a Times Ed. She looked through all the posts – Lincolnshire, Teesside, Wolverhampton. Her heart tumbled as she imagined the staffrooms, the low easy-chairs beleaguered by tables lumpy with piles of books, the rented flats in Victorian terraced houses with dank gardens. She turned to the foreign section. Most people would overlook the advert, never having heard of the island, but she knew that it was only a few hundred miles up country from her brother. He'd told her about what it was like living there, canoeing past the red and gold woods in the fall, skiing through them in the black and white of winter. If she got the job she would escape from the provincial towns of England, from a life like her head of department. It had been kind of him and his wife to ask her for dinner but the sight of the yellowing nappies on the hall radiator revealed an existence at such variance with the ebullient talent he displayed at school that it had disconcerted her, and his irrepressible laugh hadn't reassured her as he gestured towards them, and said, you'll have those one day.

She selected what she felt would be the appropriate outfit for the interview, a suit, to show that she understood the responsibilities of teaching, a cowboy hat to indicate that she was adventurous, and travelled to London determined to get the job. She was offered it, and accepted it, there and then. Before she caught the train back to the Midlands she bought her flight. She would leave making other preparations after spending her summer holidays at home.

The heat wave that had destroyed any pretence of work in the final part of the term remained unbroken, the gravel outside her mother's front door baked in the noon sun. Even quite early in the mornings it struck at her shoulders as she walked in and out of the shade of the oak trees on her way to shop, and after lunch as she drove to the beach, barefoot, wearing only her bikini and her shorts, her towel thrown onto the rear seat with the dog, it emptied the village leaving it still and quiet. As she came home in the late afternoon its rays lingered on her salty back prickling it so that she had to scrub at it with her towel.

Her mother stayed in the dining room during the day, reading the papers, the curtains drawn against the fearsome light. At last at six her mother went in to the next room to watch the news, and she herself would stop to lean against the door jamb and glance at the world's events, as she passed backwards and forwards, picking up her swimming things where they had lain to dry on the lawn, turning on the hose to water the vegetables her father had planted during his brief visit in the spring. When she had tidied away she swept the kitchen floor of the dried grass and dust that she and the dog had brought in.

The programme ended, her mother would come through and open the curtains to let in the gentler evening sunshine.

She would ask her mother what she wanted to eat, knowing that earlier she had choked down a mouthful simply to maintain the appearance of normality, but she always answered, I don't feel like anything, you make whatever you want, and so she delayed cooking until it was dusk, until it was a little cooler, so that her mother's throat would be less restricted and she could swallow some food. Sometimes, just before they ate she was able to persuade her to come outside, into the dark of the garden, so that she could feel its freshness.

At the table together they talked about what it would be like, this place, what she would need to take, what to wear in the freezing temperatures from November to April. Her mother said she would give her a fur coat.

Not fur, she said, no one wears real fur any longer. Instead she'd accept a sheepskin, so they decided that she should go and look for one at the County Show. The late August sky was hot and grey, the grass under her sandals, bruised with treading, smelt fermented. It was the wrong time of year to buy warm clothing and there was only one coat on any of the stalls which sold boots, jackets, bags, jodhpurs. It was close fitted, in the Russian style, but she slipped it on, the wool of the sleeves clasping her arms, stifling her body, and fastened the toggles and frogging. They were awkward and would be even more inconvenient in the cold, but she was thankful that it was the right size, and that her mother could participate in her preparations, so she paid for it and hooked her finger through its loop chain to carry it away. As she made her way out of the ground she stopped to watch the jumping. No one that she knew was entering, they'd all left now, and everyone was either much older or much younger than herself, nor could she see any of her mother's handful of friends amongst the spectators sitting around the ring on the bonnets of their cars or on rugs in front of them.

In the week before she left the heat became less sullen, and a breeze intermittently lifted the leaves of the trees in the orchard. The apples were beginning to look almost ready, but she knew if she bit one it would dry her mouth. She went to the village to buy the week's groceries, stamps at the post office, ham and a joint of beef at the butcher's. Hear you're off, they said, with your father abroad – it's the Middle East isn't it – that'll be all three of you out of the country. How's your brother getting on?

He's really enjoying himself, doing a lot of diving in his spare time, she said. I'm going to be near him you know.

That'll be nice for you and him. They handed her the sirloin wrapped in its smooth off-white paper. Your mother will miss you, they said. I expect she's liked having you back, seeing as she doesn't get out any longer.

She returned to the car and went on into the town to make arrangements for traveller's cheques and currency, enough to tide her over until she got paid, and some for her brother, a present to him from her mother.

Then she went to see her grandmother. They ate peppery cucumber sandwiches that bit at the tip of her tongue, and drank several cups of tea, her grandmother emptying each cup into the slop basin before refilling it. She tried to persuade her that she didn't mind having the dregs topped up, that she liked her tea tepid, that it was more refreshing that way, but her grandmother persisted in the ritual.

As he never wrote letters she told her about what her brother was doing, then about the latest event in her father's life, his short break at the Mediterranean coast, and about her own plans. Together, they puzzled over her mother's fear, wondering why it seemed to be made worse by this weather that they both so enjoyed, whether it could be overcome. They worried about her being so alone, her grandmother saying, it's so difficult for me to get up to see her now I'm no longer allowed to drive. At the gate they said goodbye, her grandmother handing her a fat bunch of sweet peas dripping water. They're for your mother, she said. I know that she loves their scent, and she realised how often they, she, her father, her brother, her grandmother, gave her mother sweets, jewellery, flowers, things to make up for their having been out, for seeing the places and meeting the people that she was cut off from. Did they give her things to placate her, to assuage her desire to get them herself, so she wouldn't want to accompany them?

That night they had supper a little earlier so that they could be cleared up by the time they rang her brother. She told him what time her plane would arrive and he said he'd come to meet her. He recounted yet another story of his risky adventures which made her laugh, but, as always, alarmed her a little. She handed the phone to her mother, who, listening to him, talking to him, became animated, telling him of the small events that made up her life, the news she garnered from the people who came to the house.

When the call was over she said to her mother, perhaps we ought to make him another birthday cake, like the one we sent last year. This time I can take it with me. I'll get the fruit tomorrow, what will we need? She went into the kitchen to find the recipe, but her mother called through, her voice flattened, it's not worth it, it's too expensive, I'll give you the money to get one out there. She came back to see that her mother's mouth had drooped, her cheerfulness transitory, deflated by the knowledge that she would only ever send things, never take them to him herself, that she would never go to visit him and her own silly desperate optimism created by her need for her mother to be happy evaporated, as she realised how her preparations for leaving would rub the wound of her mother's incarceration raw, would assert how peripheral to her husband and her children her life was. She would be careful, but she knew that her mother, in the darkened dining room, would be aware of what she was doing. She imagined that even her skin would be alert to what was happening.

The next morning she went up to the attic to get the suitcases while her mother was still asleep, bringing them down slowly, without noise, a large blue one and the soft cream-coloured one. She took them into her brother's bedroom where she would pack them. She looked at the labels from the past journeys. It shouldn't matter about those from the old steamer lines, Blue Funnel, White Star, stating ship's name, deck and cabin, but she tore off the airline ones showing destinations and flight numbers. She didn't want either her clothes or her books going to the wrong country. She closed the door to the room. If her mother saw the cases on her way downstairs after her breakfast it would blight her whole day. Not even the newspapers would be able to distract her.

She decided she'd go to the garage now to organise her taxi to Heathrow, that way she'd avoid having to tell her mother where she was going or force her to hear the details being sorted out on the phone, but she didn't want to take the dog, nor have him bark if she left him inside, so she held him by his collar and ran him up the garden to put him in the shed, the dew on the lawn tickling the sides of her feet. The air was cool, had become brisker and for the first time she began to feel a kind of anticipation. It was nearly autumn. She wanted to go.

In the tiny office on the first floor she sniffed the familiar reek of petrol and squeezed into the chair between the two desks covered as usual with untidy heaps of bills and advertisements for engine oil. She and the secretary discussed what her father was doing, the school where she would teach, whether she'd get to see her brother much, and how long it would take to get to the airport. The secretary said I'll get Brian to pick you up at seven, that'll leave you plenty of time to spare.

Seven o'clock was much too early for her mother who avoided waking until after midday if she could manage it. She would have to say goodbye to her the night before. Her mother would be better able to cope then. She felt ashamed that she was so relieved, that she wouldn't have to watch her mother almost unable to speak, gagged by her attempts to appear not terrified, and desolate at losing her too.

I'll charge it to your mother as usual, shall I? I don't suppose there'll be anyone coming to stay with her? It's going to be lonely for her, she'll miss you. The secretary's face was kind, concerned for her mother.

I know, she said, but what can I do? She got up and clattered down the narrow wooden stairs, her guilt accompanying her along the road. The chill had gone but the sun no longer had its strength, no longer stunning her mind as she had allowed it to all summer, no longer annihilating the worry. She could pull out of the job, it was very late to do so, but she'd done something like it once before when she'd been working in Madrid. She had been so desperate to leave that she'd told them a half lie, that her mother was sick, that she needed to return to look after her.

Coming in through the open front door she found her mother sitting reading. I'll get the lunch, she said, and went into the kitchen. She cleaned radishes, scraped carrots, cut bread and laid cold meat on two plates. She came in to put out knives, forks. I've arranged the car for Tuesday. It'll be here at seven. Her mother groaned, laid down *The Times* and opened *The Telegraph*. You needn't get up to see me off, she said. Her mother didn't reply. She stood in the doorway opposite her. Do you want me to stay? If I stayed you could get some treatment, we could take it little by little, go a tiny bit further each time. In a year you might be able to get out on your own.

Her mother continued to stare at the print. At last she understood that her mother didn't want to be helped because that would mean leaving the safe walls of her home.

She hadn't brought the butter in.

She didn't want to go and be responsible for her mother's loneliness, and she couldn't remain here, sharing her mother's terror. She didn't want to be sad for her and it wasn't fair, but she had to say it. They think in the village that I should stay to look after you.

Her mother raised her head and looked at her through glasses that magnified her grey-green eyes. Of course you must go, she said.

Wardrobe

The little white tin is an
oval cameo.
A hole inside it,
it clasps what it holds
catches and keeps it.

An old lady shakily
picks it up
strokes it, makes it shiny.
It's her secret.
She keeps within –

The wardrobe dark
where the clothes hang
Forever waiting.

The smell of melted mothballs
coating the coats,
the skirts.
The shoes that lie below.

She drops it –
A tinkly clang –
turns her head
swiftly, guiltily.

The empty hallway
reflects the black room.

She picks up the tin
opens it
inside
is an ear lobe
as green and ghastly
as the old man she killed.

Gillian Appleby

THE BULL

Andrew Hurley

The three soldiers found the village in ruins.

They had seen many like this: roads pitted with huge craters, trees blown apart, houses reduced to low brick squares that looked like Roman remains.

Sometimes they found survivors or the buildings still smoking but this village was cold. There had been no fighting here for weeks. Bloated bodies lay on the main road that ran through the village and out into the country on the other side: a few old people too weak or too proud to run away, covered in autumn leaves and the grime splashed out of the puddles in which they lay.

Phillips prodded one of the corpses with the end of his rifle and the others watched, then they carried on along the main street to the church in the village square.

The front half of the church was missing – a bomb had come through the roof and blown the front and most of the side walls outwards. The soldiers looked down the central aisle at an enormous pit in the floor from which the remains of pews, pillars and flagstones radiated. The roof of the church had collapsed almost entirely leaving a few rafters jutting into the sky, and the three soldiers watched as rainwater dripped from them into puddles and onto the painted statues that lay stiffly in the rubble.

On the back wall was the framework of a stained glass window, emptied of its colours, around which a fresco of angels had been fading for a hundred years. Beneath this, a huge, splintered wooden crucifix leaned precariously over the altar; one of the chains that held it in place had been ripped from the wall.

"There's not much hope for us if they got Him, is there?" Anderson said.

Phillips had his rifle up to his shoulder and was looking through the sight. He took it down and said, "What do we do now?"

Jackson, who was the senior in rank, told them to search for bodies.

Phillips went one way and Anderson the other, climbing onto mounds of rubble that extended into the graveyard where headstones had been shattered or thrown against the blackened stumps of cypress trees. The soldiers worked quickly, turning over lumps of concrete and brick with their hands, their rifles slung around their backs.

They found nothing living and moved further in.

At the front of the church they came across a piano covered in brick dust. Phillips flipped open the lid and dabbed at the keys.

Anderson righted a triptych that had fallen on the floor and folded. He opened it out and looked at the paintings: Christ being crucified, Mary weeping, Christ ascending into heaven.

Phillips noticed Anderson looking at the paintings. "Do you know how fast Christ would have had to have gone to get to heaven?" he said, playing the last three notes on the piano in triplets.

"What are you talking about?" Anderson said.

"They've worked out how fast you have to go to leave the Earth," Phillips replied.

"Do you think it applies to the Son of God?" said Anderson, wiping dust of the canvases with his sleeve.

"Seven miles a second," Phillips said. "That's how fast Jesus needed to go."

Anderson shook his head and as Phillips went back to the piano he began to follow the Stations of the Cross around the church, clambering over the piles of earth and stone. The first four were hidden in the rubble so that the Passion began with Simon carrying the cross to Golgotha and continued until Jesus was nailed to the cross. Anderson studied the wooden carving of the slumped Christ and the women at his feet and the words '*Eloi, Eloi lama sabachthani*' painted in a Gothic script below. He looked for the last two stations but they were buried.

"Come here," Jackson said and the two soldiers went over to where he was standing with his rifle pointing down a hole in the floor.

"What's down there?" Phillips asked.

"The crypt," said Anderson.

"Look down," Jackson said and stepped aside so that they could see.

Half way down the steps a bull lay dead. The stone walls and the steps were covered in dried blood. The bull seemed to fill the stairwell. Had it fallen any further it would have blocked the doorway at the bottom completely.

"Jesus," Phillips whispered.

"It must have wandered in from the farm up the road," Anderson said.

"Why would it do that?" Phillips asked.

They descended the steps in single file, stepping between the bull's broken legs and then clambered over its head. Anderson, who was last, stopped and put his hands around the horns. Their tips were covered in blood. Anderson touched the tips with his thumbs.

"They've been sharpened," he said.

"Why do they do that?" Phillips asked from the bottom of the steps.

"For fighting," Anderson replied. "It's a fine animal," he said and patted the bull's side, feeling the muscles hard like overlapping sandbags beneath the black skin.

The door at the bottom of the steps was open and Jackson stepped into the crypt with his finger poised over the trigger of his rifle.

"Anyone there?" he shouted. There was no reply. "Phillips," Jackson said. "Bring that light in here."

Phillips took off his pack and undid the straps that held a storm lantern tight against the canvas. He gave it to Anderson while he took out some matches, lit the wick and closed the glass door. Jackson took the lantern and, bringing its light into the crypt, saw the body of a man on the floor, his arms spread out, his eyes fixed on the ceiling, a shotgun diagonal across his chest. Jackson stepped over the body and with his neck bent under the low ceiling went to the back of the crypt, illuminating the shapes of stacked coffins and recesses in the walls where candles had burned down to coins of wax.

Anderson and Phillips lingered by the doorway looking at the body, their hands cupped over their noses. Jackson looked at them from the other side of the room and then came over.

"I don't know if it's him or the bull that smells the worst," Phillips said.

"Pick up the gun," Jackson said.

Anderson knelt down and took the gun off the man's chest. He broke it open, saw a single cartridge left inside and showed it to Jackson.

"Christ almighty," Phillips mumbled turning away.

Jackson and Anderson looked back at the body. An inch-deep ridge ran from the top of the man's left thigh to his right shoulder, crossing his stomach where the flesh at the edges of the gash turned inwards. Through the rips in the man's shirt they could see where his ribs had been exposed.

"Cover him up with one of those sheets." Jackson indicated a pile of shrouds that were heaped against the back wall and gave Anderson the lantern.

Phillips went back up the steps and Jackson followed him.

Anderson put the lantern down, picked up the uppermost sheet and took it over to the body. He thought about putting the body in one of the coffins but didn't want to search for an empty one. He covered the body with the sheet and saw it was too short. The man's boots stuck out; battered farmer's boots with nail ends in the soles.

Anderson noticed the spent cartridge next to the man's body and picked it up. Then he went back up the stairs, stopping by the bull and lifting its head. A hole in its throat was plugged with congealed blood that smelt of soil.

When he got back up to the church Jackson was urinating next to the lectern, and Phillips had the piano lid open again and was stabbing out the three chords that he had learned as a child.

Nicola Scargill

I stared into the tiny red point of light over my head, into my own recorded self on the small video screen.

"Dear Diary…" The playback sounded nasal, whiny. It cut off after a few minutes. The eye hadn't seen that thing with Montgomery.

I lay back on the bed, on the sheets that smelled old and slept in, comfy. One side was covered in red goo, the stuff that had come out of Montgomery when his skin burst and a big green bug was lying where the blonde senior I'd been playing Kick The Can with a few hours ago had been.

In the hours before Mel got with Surf and Ski and Lucifer bawled them all out in Jujifruit's den. Before Ducky threw himself screaming into the pool at the same party and Dingbat had to jump in with her corndog half eaten and pull him up to give him mouth to mouth. Before that weird Elvis guy Alyssa hangs out with beat a guy to death with a can of soup and Cowboy cried 'cause Bart killed himself watching the televangelist on TV.

The screen fuzzed up before it played the Valley girls at the bus shelter, all big hair and platform shoes with matching accessorised shades in red, blue and green. The alien was still there across the street looking like Godzilla in all those movies where Tokyo gets crushed by a lizard with an attitude. I'd got their babbling in the background, Thomas and Eileen and whoever else was going to some party they weren't gonna get to anytime soon. I didn't get them being vaporised, just the seat they'd been sat on vacated except for three sets of headgear.

I lit up a smoke and watched it again wishing I'd got their faces when the ray gun hit them.

The TV clicked on and I was staring down the barrel of God and his messengers. The guy had to be in his forties and had had a few yanks round the hairline down the road. His eyes were small and too bright, but it was a cold light they had, like a star on a frosty night. With his white suit and weird black haircut he looked like that singer Elvis was named after, like a sleazy Vegas hustler sniffing a buck. Espresso and froot loops I'd chewed 12 hours ago started to wriggle in my gut.

"I cannot hear you brothers and sisters…" I could see my shadow on the screen, like a smear on the preacher's face. The smoke glowed on his forehead like the sights of a semi-automatic.

Ducky's sister stuck her head in the microwave. Just came home, watched some TV and nuked her brains out while the family watched *Wheel of Fortune* in the next room. She was at the café this morning with Alyssa and Dingbat, scarfing cake before class and puking it before tardies. She would have bought it the same time Bart did, maybe the same time Handjob's heart spat up the last chunks of blood on the beer and corn nuts in the kitchen. It's been a shitty week.

Montgomery was this guy in our class I'd seen around. He had these gorgeous eyes, blue and green, one of each, and blonde hair that curled up around his neck. He was real pale, sort of nervous, real quiet. I used to think about him sometimes when Mel was out with Lucifer or one of her skags. We picked him up for breakfast and he started babbling about the rapture, going even paler than usual and bolting like a bunny rabbit. I found his cross at Kick The Can in the locker room after the same lizard from the shelter got him with a souped up water pistol. It shook me a bit. Then he knocked on my window maybe half an hour ago with a goddamn sucker pad on his forehead.

I wasn't sure if the thing that crawled out on six legs was him or an alien pod.

"…It's like I got cotton balls in my ears…" The preacher kept at it, yellow letters scrolling the bottom of the screen to tell me what number to call if I wanted to make a donation to the cause. "Get a picture of Heaven nice and clear in your minds/Ain't it nice? Ain't it so gosh darn wonderful?" The letters started to change colours as the preacher talked with his audience. Bart's mom called in and started raving in Swedish about her son and how the show had subliminal messages telling kids to kill themselves before The Judgement. There were subtitles in little red letters under the picture of Christ on the horizon.

I put my hand on the phone, suddenly wanting to call that number and tell the preacher that my girlfriend was out with a pair of twins and a guy I saw get vaporised by aliens had climbed in my window while I was in bed and turned into a bug.

It rang under my hand, the jolts shooting up my arm and knocking my smoke out of my hand.

"Dark?"

"Yeah." It was Mel. They hadn't zapped her yet.

"You okay?" She sounded strung out, like her vocal chords were wound too tight.

"Never better." I could see her making big eyes at me and wrapping her hair around her finger, stretching the curl out to watch it snap back.

"That's good. Okay if I come over? Lucifer's being a total dork about Surf and Ski. She knows my take on that stuff."

"Pass it around before you're old, right?"

"Right. So can I come over?" I looked up at the ceiling, at the painting I did in grey; me and a gun. And shrugging:

"Sure."

"Great. There in five, K?"

"Yeah. Great." I dropped the phone, let it sink into a green mess that might have been a sandwich before the bacteria got it and it started to glow in the dark.

Bart's mom had been cut off while I was on the line and now there was a girl crying on air about her Buddhist boyfriend who would burn in hell after the rapture was over.

The red eye blinked on and my face filled up the screen, big dark eyes and too pale skin like a death rocker without the sense of humour.

"We believe…" The audience were chanting it now like one big sheep in total unison with their shepherd. On the screen, pale lips shaped the words.

"We believe…"

The picture stared down at me. The .45 came from nowhere, sitting in my hand like a bug on a windshield.

"We believe." And on the screen the boy cocked the gun to his left temple, and he smiled like the televangelist on TV, like he knew something everyone else was in the dark about.

"We believe."

THE PAPER CRANE MAN: NI (TWO)

Katy Harrison

5th August 2005, 19:59:03, Hiroshima, Japan

The plane touched down at Hiroshima's main airport 40 kilometres east of the city. As it shuddered and graunched its way to a standstill Kiyoshi's stomach hitched toward his mouth. He gripped the armrests and tried to look as calm as possible. He held his bag to him, taking care to create a shell for it with his arms. It would be devastating if its contents were to get this far only to be crushed in an aeroplane landing.

Without luggage to collect from the carousel, Kiyoshi boarded a bus to the railway station.

At the station Kiyoshi decided to eat before he went into the city centre. He found a *shokudÿ* and stared at its lurid plastic food displays in the window before entering. It was reasonably quiet and the waiter who was wiping tables looked up as Kiyoshi pushed open the door. He flipped his cloth over his shoulder and approached Kiyoshi.

'Nan-mei sama?'

Kiyoshi held up one finger to indicate that it would just be him eating. The waiter led him to a table at the back of the restaurant and brought him a hot towel, a cup of tea and the menu. Kiyoshi wiped his hands and face with the towel and tried to get rid of the tiredness that seemed to ingrain itself like dirt into the folds and wrinkles of his skin. When the waiter returned he ordered *hiroshima-yaki*, the local speciality of pancakes made with *soba*, the thin buckwheat noodles, and fried egg.

His food arrived quickly. Pressing his hands together he said *'Itadakimasu'* meaning 'I will humbly receive this food,' a Shinto tradition that shows respect for the meal and any loss of life that may have come to pass in the making of it.

He ate with disposable chopsticks, savouring the taste in each bite. His waiter continued to wipe down tables and take orders from the smattering of other customers. Occasionally he would look over at Kiyoshi, who in turn wondered how he appeared to the young waiter with his long dyed-brown hair.

He no doubt looked older than his 66, almost 67, years with his carved wrinkles and thinning hair. He was probably wondering what such an old man was doing eating alone in a *shokudÿ*. He was obviously not a salaryman; his suit was not expensive enough or well cared for. He didn't look at his watch or rush his food, so he had nowhere important to be. The bag with his precious cargo was a shabby one, clearly from the country. For some reason, to Kiyoshi it mattered what this young waiter thought of him. It mattered that he wasn't just seen as a faceless face in the crowd, as an outsider.

Kiyoshi finished his food and tea and signalled for the bill by making an X with two fingers. He paid in cash, slowly counting out the *yen* notes before leaving the restaurant. He boarded a streetcar and began heading for the city centre.

The waiter in the restaurant approached the table where Kiyoshi had eaten intending to wipe it down. He saw that the old man had left something behind. A perfect white *origami* crane was placed in the centre of the table. The waiter stared at it for a moment, understanding. Then he gently picked it up and put it behind the counter, saving it for the following day.

6th August 2005, 06:37:54

Kiyoshi spent the night in a cheap hotel just west of the *Hon-dori Arcade*, a strip of road that clattered non-stop with the rush of busy shoppers and entertainment hunters. He woke as the sun came up. It was a beautiful day, much as it had been 60 years before. How was it that such a huge amount of time, practically a lifetime, could seem so short? How was it that just by closing his eyes he was right back in his parents' house, getting ready for school, six years old and full of excitement?

Kiyoshi checked out of his room around seven. He was wearing the same clothes that he had worn the day before. His bag was slung over one shoulder and despite being packed to bursting, it felt as light as feathers. On his way, Kiyoshi passed by the remnants of an old building. Only the steps and the crumbling boundary wall indicated that anything had ever stood there. Etched on the stone steps was the shadow of a vaporised man who had sat there only seconds before the bomb. From where he was stood Kiyoshi could see where his knee, his feet, his body would have been angled to create the outline. There was no trace of the man himself, not even a plaque.

08:09:32

Kiyoshi arrived at the *Heiwa-kÿen* (Peace Memorial Park) a little after eight to find the green space filled with people, most sitting in provided seats but more standing behind. For some reason he hadn't expected it to be so busy, but salarymen, housewives, *yanqui*, children, the elderly – it seemed as if all of Hiroshima had turned out for the anniversary. Yet despite the sheer volume of people, the air was not filled with excited chatterings or people shouting to be heard over others. People talked, yes, but it was shockingly quiet.

This was not a tourist attraction; this was clearly a memorial.

It was odd seeing the calm of all these people. Only yesterday, as he walked down the *Hon-dori Arcade,* had Kiyoshi been stunned by the noise and rush of a modern Japanese city. The *ko gyaru*, teenage school girls in miniskirts with dark suntans, strode confidently around the *yanqui* who chattered into their mobile phones, barely noticing them. The salarymen, already drunk and headed to karaoke bars, stared after the school girls and a group of Office Ladies walking the other way tutted loudly.

Kiyoshi had been transfixed by this absurd pantomime, beneath the clatter of arcade machines, digital music and restaurant owners calling from the door. This couldn't really be the way people were here, so alien, so ridiculous. It was hard to imagine that these were the same people sitting quietly in the *Heiwa-kÿen*.

08:15:00

At exactly 8:15 the Bell of Peace rang out. When the deep tolling had stopped every siren in the city went off. Chills went through Kiyoshi's body as burglar alarms, ambulance sirens, car anti-theft devices and air-raid alerts flooded the quiet and rose into the sky in a deafening shriek. When the noise stopped the minute's silence began.

Kiyoshi felt the whole experience of the bombing run through him in a jolt.

The flash, the heat baking their skin.

He had relived it every day since it had happened, but being back home, seeing the rebuilt city standing on what had been nothing but a death zone, hit him hard.

The cloud that transfixed them, so strange and simple rising into the sky.

He felt sick, but knew this time it wasn't radiation. It was something else; an intrinsic sadness that he knew had always been there, but which he'd refused to acknowledge.

The rolling black cloud that destroyed everything in its path, then finally the blast hitting the school and throwing everything to the floor.

He thought of his mother and father. He thought too, of his uncle and aunt, now dead some ten years. He thought too late of how much they had done for him and how little he had given to them. Not all of those orphaned by the bomb were lucky enough to have relatives to take them in.

Carbonised bodies in piles, the injured crawling over limbs and rubble.

As the minute's silence ended, the stillness in the park persisted. The gathered crowd did not break into talk of their day, of others, of things they would do. Visiting Hiroshima for the first time since the bombing, Kiyoshi could see how the city had been affected. He could see people like himself, rooted to the spot and staring out at something others could not see.

The cries and groans for water, – 'Mizú! Sumímasen, mizú!' – and the soldiers carrying water flasks walking through the devastation.

He could see young people dressed in flashy clothes and arrogance now devoid of banter. They, too, were clearly remembering. Family they had never met, perhaps. Maybe their city that would forever be overshadowed by a sense of loss and dread.

His mother, her skin tattered and sore, cold and stiff.

Or perhaps, more simply, they remembered the lives of others.

09:47:42

When Kiyoshi felt he was ready he made his way across the park to the Children's Peace Memorial. While people were still nearby, it was quieter than perhaps it would have been at 8:15. A cluster of children, shaven-headed and deformed stood with their carers nearby; their DNA twisted by the radiation that had contaminated their parents and grandparents.

Strung around the curving missile-shaped memorial, topped with a statue of a child reaching to the sky, were lines of brightly coloured cranes. Lines of red, blue, green, pink, yellow, white, orange and purple paper birds crowded around the perimeter edge of the monument. They had been sent from all over Japan as a declaration of peace and a monument to the dead children of 1945.

When Kiyoshi found a suitable spot, slightly secluded from the other people, he knelt and undid his bag, from which he took 992 white *origami* cranes. Gently he placed them one by one at a corner of the piles of cranes. When he had finished, Kiyoshi stood and pressed the palms of his hands together. He remained like this for a few moments and when he looked up he could see the waiter from the *shokudÿ* he had visited yesterday. He was approaching the monument and had not seen or had not recognised Kiyoshi, who watched as he placed the crane Kiyoshi had folded with the others. He, too, had a moment of silence before turning and leaving.

Then came a girl from the hotel Kiyoshi had stayed at the night before, the maid who had cleaned his room. She, too, carried a crane, which she had discovered on the floor in the middle of the room after he had left.

Then the man who had sat beside Kiyoshi on the bus. Only after Kiyoshi had alighted did the man look up from his paper to find the crane on the seat next to him.

The air steward who had checked the plane that had flown Kiyoshi to Hiroshima airport and found a crane nestled in the overhead storage compartment.

The shopkeeper who discovered a crane sitting on a shelf in between inch-thick *manga* comics that Kiyoshi had looked at on his way to the hotel the day before.

The passer-by who noticed a crane sitting on the ruined steps of an old scorched building.

The woman who had helped Kiyoshi to his feet when he stumbled on the busy modern roads and had found a crane tucked into her handbag when she reached for her purse.

And finally the little boy, his hand folded in his mother's, cradling a crane that an old man had given him to stop him crying.

One crane for each decade, plus two more for his parents.

None of those who bore the paper birds to the memorial recognised Kiyoshi.

11:19:12

The A-Bomb Memorial loomed in front of him.

The skeletal roof and shattered foundations sat quietly in front of the Motoyasu river, unthreatening and desecrated. The frame of the dome was reduced to spindly girders that clawed the sky like fingers.

In a flash Kiyoshi saw the building in flames, terrifying as it squatted among the remains of the city. The heat was everywhere and everything was doused in grey and red. Bleeding burnt bodies lay twisted among rubble and steel. Screams and smoke and a boiling river.

Another flash and Kiyoshi was back. Birds called and he caught the scent of the *ginkgo* trees. The dome was no longer horrible; now it was just empty. He wondered where exactly his father had died and how close he might have been to finding him before he collapsed.

21:17:41

When night fell hundreds gathered outside the A-Bomb Dome, which glowed green under floodlights. All were clutching paper lanterns inscribed with messages of remembrance. One by one they were lit and gently lowered onto the surface of the river. An array of colour bobbed downstream, the softly glowing lights contrasting against the neon and headlights of the modern city in the east.

Heads face down in the water and faces staring skyward. Eyes frozen, the tiniest movement in the river as the undercurrent nudged the crush of bodies.

Kiyoshi shook his head. No, there were only lanterns in the river now. No dead bodies here.

Tourists, photographers and those there to remember gathered to watch the annual Lantern Floating Memorial. One lantern for each of the dead, a traditional Japanese farewell caught in the twenty-first century. The lanterns gently rode the current of the river in which so many had sought refuge in after the blast, only to find it poisonous.

Kiyoshi watched the event with tired eyes. The day was winding down and soon it would be the next day. Tomorrow there would be nothing to commemorate, nothing to remember. It would be an ordinary day in the city and those who had passed the hours today with such reverence would return to their normal routine of work and play. Companies would expect their employees to arrive on time. Shopkeepers would expect deliveries and customers. Schoolchildren would be expected to know their times tables.

The world would go on.

An extract from a longer story.

Sign Her Out

Just one cataract clouded eye,
The left eye stripped in a laser flash,
Watching us, laughing at the kids
"That little one's funny!"

Not a clue who that little one is.

A dog dark, dun black Labrador woman
Gone white and veil thin.
Matron frame and buffed tar kabuki hair
Reduced to slouch and hump. Pale now
        Lame.

Just the one cataract clouded eye.
The other, wet as an otter's,
Scans the room; finds no peace at home
Not now all our names have petered out and gone.

Gone, how to bake, to scramble an egg.
Gone, who bought the clay duck on the ledge?
Gone, who we were, from that mollusc egg,
Calcified. Set in skin.

This paper white muffin case woman, a
Prototype me. A mother. Widow.
Dimmed by a squishy white mantle,
Burgled, doctor prodded (senile old girl).

At the end she goes back to the home,
Soaked in the seat with her own bitter piss.

Only one cataract clouded eye –
The left as fast as a bee. On the nightstand
A cup of pills, a photo of her Bill.

2 children (one son, one daughter)
6 grandchildren
3 great grandchildren
After him the rot took hold,
Causing endless lists.
Now she can't remember
Who Bill is.

Rebecca Allen

She did not feel
it crawl into her breast;
only knew it was there from
the shape on the scan. A grainy

starfish; just a cluster of suckers
and selfish cells, no heart
or backbone; it wanted
to take hers. When

they tried
to cut it out,
a sly tentacle slipped
beyond the scalpel's reach.

It wriggled away, anemone-slick,
to re-generate with slow malice;
to re-appear a year after the
all-clear. And the drugs,

indiscriminate killers, dragged
in a failed catch; her own
tissue hooked, while
metastases passed

through the net, drifting
like plankton, through her blood –
finding new vessels to settle inside.
As she softened and weakened with each

pull of the tide, she sensed him waiting,
dark and flat-shelled, on the horizon;
came to recognise his sea-eyes
in the red blink of the

machines that kept her alive;
heard the death-rattle of his claws on
hospital floors. And when he began to chip
at her limbs with cold pincers, loosening

her hold on the rocks – she let the ocean
guide her, kicking further from land
with each morphine click, felt his black
strength beside her as she swam.

CONSTANCE AND THE ANGEL

Roz Clarke

It is half an hour after midnight. I am alone. This rarely happens; Harry is undergoing his treatment, and Felicity is on solo shift. She has gone to the bathroom. There is no camera in the bathroom.

Thinking about being alone, I look for lonely people. If I pull back, relax my focus, I can feel them as a mass, a blur, and it's as though I can sense their thoughts, though of course I can no more do this than Harry or Sarah or Felicity, watching individuals on their grainy screens. I have told them about this feeling. They theorise, I don't listen.

I don't know what loneliness feels like from the inside; to me it's a hundred thousand people sitting alone with that look on their faces, disconnected. Lost. The feeling threatens to overwhelm me, and I ride it for a few seconds, horribly curious – is this despair? Is this bitterness? The ones that cry don't trouble me as much as the ones with the dead faces.

One holds my attention, and I bring her into focus. A young Aunt, recently confirmed in her order, sits alone in a candle-lit chapel. I know her; I review my memories.

Constance at 15, laughing with friends in a schoolroom, grey sweater and brown slacks, blonde hair swinging.

Constance laughing in a red and blue lit room, uncurling her hand to reveal two luminous green lozenges, thrusting them into her mouth.

Constance at 17, painting a devotional image, her hand tracing a line of colour along the back of Malcolm Makepeace's black coat, a dark blue sky that she will later dot with stars, taking her time, positioning each one just so.

Constance two months later, standing in a doorway, the body of her father lying across the floor at her feet, his hand outstretched. Heart attack. She doesn't weep.

Constance signing her Declaration of Faith and Devotion. Constance having her hair pinned beneath a white cloth, her knuckles white around the cold steel of the double M that she will wear on a chain around her throat for the rest of her life.

Now she sits alone in a candle-lit chapel, and she has that dead look.

Someone enters behind her, but Constance doesn't stir. Ah, I have been waiting for this.

The newcomer walks up behind Constance and touches her shoulder. A deep and warm voice softly says her name.

Constance gradually focuses her gaze on the candle in front of her.

—Yes? Please, I am at prayer.

—So late? What troubles you?

—I am not troubled, friend. Must I be troubled, in order to pray?

There is a flaw in Constance's voice, the tiniest crack in the edge of a glass.

With a show of reluctance, she turns her head. Instead of white robes, she finds smooth, bare knees, and she is forced to crane her neck back, passing her eyes over a short golden tunic hanging in loose folds, to a face. It is an ineffable face. Neither young nor old, male nor female, kind nor cruel. The tawny eyes speak of ancient wisdom, but the mouth has a flippant curve.

—Stand up, child, so we may speak as equals.

The stranger holds out both hands and helps Constance to her feet.

—I know you are troubled Constance. I've been watching you. If you are ready to confess what grieves your heart, I will listen. If you are not, then I will wait, and watch, until the right time comes. You are not alone.

—Who are you?

—You can think of me as your guardian angel, if you like.

Constance shakes her head. At first I think it's denial, but when she looks up again her eyes are full of wonder.

—Or you don't have to think of me at all.

The angel reaches out an elegant hand and strokes her cheek; a tear starts in Constance's eye and rolls down, splashing the long fingers.

—But I do so hope you will think of me sometimes.

—I can't, Constance exclaims. You're a– It doesn't make any sense. There are no such things as angels. We left all that nonsense behind when we left–

—Earth, yes, yes, I know. Blessed Makepeace and his so-tidy orthodoxy.

—I don't know what you mean.

—Of course you don't, dear one, of course you don't. I'm sorry. I didn't mean to upset you.

The angel folds Constance in strong, gleaming arms, and presses her head to its shoulder. After a moment, Constance raises her head; both eyes are glistening now. The angel wipes moisture away with a tender fingertip.

—Now, can you put your hand on your heart and tell me you're not grieving?

Constance shakes her white-folded head.

—And it's not for the death of you father alone, is it?

The angel takes Constance's right hand in its left, and places both over Constance's heart.

—Better yet, put your hand on my heart.

It takes both their hands and transfers them to its own breast. The candles in the room begin to gutter; the dance of the shadows on the walls becomes frantic. The stranger's skin takes on a golden luminescence, and the air beats with the velvet pressure of unseen wings.

Cloth of gold is swept aside; hands are pressed against hot flesh. Constance is still weeping. She pulls back her hand, but the gesture is weak. Briefly, the angel's breast lies bare; full, round, hard-tipped in russet brown.

Constance's hand is drawn across this glowing dark-eyed orb, until it is obscured by her fingers, fingers pressed down and, this time, held hard.

Constance whispers something, too soft for my pickups to catch.

The angel looses its right hand from around her waist, and tilts her chin up.

—What's that, love?

—I always thought– Constance falters.

—You thought angels didn't exist? I know. I'm trying not to take offence, don't worry.

—No. I thought, that if they existed, they would be, that is, they wouldn't have–

The angel tips its head back and laughs.

—You thought angels would be sexless? Oh, my darling girl. Well, it seems we both have a confession to make.

The golden stranger takes Constance's hand and slips it under its short tunic skirt. Lips brush together and then meet in a kiss.

—How did you know? Constance murmurs.

—I have watched over you. I know your heart.

The angel takes Constance's hand and moves it further up beneath the tunic. Constance's eyebrows lift and her mouth falls open. The angel closes her mouth with another kiss, soft and lingering. Fleetingly, I wonder how it must feel to have skin, and lips, and a tongue to probe with. All the poetry in the library is mine for the taking, all the romances, but they mean less to me than the town shellfish report. Will I ever understand? They have promised me pressure sensors, but without desire, I shan't feel what these two are feeling, skin-drenched with rosy flame.

They sink to the floor, and I hear a whisper; I cannot see their mouths any more but I know whose lips the verse springs from, and I know the verse though it's spoken too gently for me to hear:

There are two Hearts whose movements thrill,
In unison so closely sweet,
That Pulse to Pulse responsive still
They Both must heave, or cease to beat.

There is no more talking.

The rest of the Aunts in the convent are sleeping, praying in their cells, reading, religiously masturbating.

In an alleyway outside a club in the Fringe, an old man is laying unconscious, blood spreading through the thin hair on his scalp.

In Fat Erik's the staff are playing dice at the only table not forested with stool legs.

—Malory, take a look at camera 4291, would you?

—(I am Grace!) Of course, Felicity.

A puffy-faced woman is sitting in a room lit only by the blue glow of her commscreen. She is watching the Night Services. She takes frequent sips from a bottle of liquor at her side. The team are not supposed to use this facility to watch their friends and relations. Felicity and I keep this secret. This is Felicity's mother. Tonight's vigil will be long, but I can keep an eye on the things that interest me, too. Quietly, a corner of my awareness remains in the candle-lit chapel, where gold and white commingle amid the susurration of wings and sleeping virgins, until Constance is carried to her bed, to wake alone with feathers in her mouth.

An extract from Roz's novel The Boa Constrictor.

Our lights
are going out

all over
the country.

We are drying up,
fading out,

and blowing away.

Let's meet here,
in the old house

after
we're dead.

There's a place for you
in the attic,

a place for me
in the shed.

Our invisible feet
will creak the floor,

our laughter an echo,
mistaken for the wind.

Sarah Hardman

Confiding in Winter

Snow fell in Fallowfield so we played with effort,
childhoods balled within our hands. You knew mine,
and I yours. We stayed a while in the cold
as the sky split into gifts and the land
hid its litter beneath the sheet.

I watched your tears fall beside the flakes
as our foot steps softened
and light doubled off the white robes
that clung to a scattering of trees.

We breathed some words amongst the asterisks
and all turned to acres of blank pages.

Sean Dagan Wood

CREDITS

MUSE is the Writing School's yearbook of creative work by students from the Manchester Metropolitan University.

Rebecca Allen, Helen Brown, Charlotte Anne Clegg and Christopher Myers are students on the BA English degree, from which Cathyrn Freear and Nicola Scargill have just graduated.

Stuart Cannell and Oliver Janson are studying on the BA English and American Literature programme.

Jessica Greaves and Alison Jeapes are on the BA in English and Creative Writing, which Katy Harrison and Sean Dagan Wood have just completed.

Michelle Fryer is studying for a BA in Humanities and Social Science.

Gillian Appleby, Roz Clarke, Mike Dugdale, Andrew Hurley and Caroline Moir are on the MA Creative Writing: Novel programme, which Rachel Broady, Katie Jukes, Gemma Kenyon and Susan Stern have just finished. Anne Louise Kershaw and Carley Moulton are from the MA Creative Writing: Poetry route.

Sarah Hardman, Glenis Stott and John Holding are Virtual Writing School students from the online MA Creative Writing: Novel programme, while Victoria Adderley is on the online Poetry route.

Paul Clayton and Katie Popperwell are studying for an MA in Critical Theory.

MUSE 5 was edited by Gillian Appleby, James Draper, Cathryn Freear, Jessica Greaves, Oliver Janson, Carley Moulton, Christopher Myers and Nicola Scargill. With special thanks to Alf Louvre and Kaye Tew for advice and support.

Design and artwork by Steve Kelly, MMU Design Studio.

Printed by Angela Cole and staff, MMU Reprographics.

For further details, or to order additional copies of *MUSE* 5, please contact:
James Draper, Project Manager: Writing School
Department of English
Manchester Metropolitan University
Tel: + 44 (0) 161 247 1787
E-mail: j.draper@mmu.ac.uk
Website: www.mmu.ac.uk/english

5 . 2006